F.A.T.E. 4

Enemy Within The Skull

Enemy Within The Skull

A F.A.T.E. Novel
by
Gregory Kern

MEWS BOOKS
LONDON AND CONNECTICUT

Also by Gregory Kern in this series:

F.A.T.E. 1: Galaxy of the Lost
F.A.T.E. 2: Slave Ship from Sergan
F.A.T.E. 3: Monster of Metelaze

This work was originally published in the U.S.A. as
CAP KENNEDY No. 4 ENEMY WITHIN THE SKULL

Copyright © 1974 by DAW BOOKS, INC.
First published in United States of America by Daw Books, January 1974

*

FIRST MEWS EDITION JULY 1976

*

Mews Books are published by
Mews Books Limited, 20 Bluewater Hill, Westport, Connecticut 06880
and distributed by
New English Library Limited, Barnard's Inn, Holborn, London EC1N 2JR.
Made and printed in Great Britain by Hunt Barnard Printing Ltd., Aylesbury, Bucks.

45200027 0

CHAPTER ONE

The site had been carefully chosen, a tiny valley thickly ringed
with trees, a lake in the center on which swans glided. The sun
was warm with a soft crimson light, the sward dotted with
flowers, the air fresh and scented with growing things. To the
hundred men and women scattered around it was an idyllic
contrast to the bleak walls and barred windows they had re-
cently known. They milled, a little unsure, not yet believing
what they had been told. On Merah prisoners were not accustomed to such treatment. They served short, harsh, savage
sentences. Rehabilitation was just a word. And yet here they
were, not a guard to be seen, low tables piled with food and
containers of wine. A party to reward them for good behavior.
A taste of freedom to remind them of the benefits of obeying
the law.

Subjects in an interesting experiment.

Ipoh-Luang was impatient. 'Why do they not begin?' he
asked. 'You would think that to such creatures the sight of food
and wine would be an instant spur.'

'They are suspicious.' Kota Bassein was just as impatient, but
age had taught him to mask his feelings. He stood in the observation dome resting on a high tripod beyond the screen of
trees. From his vantage point he could see what the prisoners
could not, the double ring of armed guards, the fence of
electrified wire. 'You must remember they are criminals and
have a highly developed sense of caution. They cannot really
believe what they see, food, wine, a day from the confines of
their cells.'

'We should have starved them for a few days. Hunger would
have driven them.'

'It would have made them even more suspicious,' corrected
Bassein. He lifted binoculars to his eyes. At the edge of the

5

lake a burly man was throwing scraps of food to the swans. 'See? They are testing it for poison.'

'They will find none.' The third occupant of the observation dome was a Chambodian. He was taller than the others, leaner, black hair sweeping in a pronounced widow's peak from a high forehead. His face was wedge-shaped, the nose beaked, the mouth a thin slit above a sloping jaw. His eyes were deepset, slanted, the irises horizontal slots. An alien whose ancestors had risen from avian, not primate stock. He wore fabric of fine-meshed scales. His hands, long-nailed, were like claws. 'The food is innocuous and they are unable to test the wine. Even if they could they would find nothing.'

'So you say.' Ipoh Luang was uneasy at the Chambodian's presence. Merah should go its own way and be dependent on no other race. And yet progress had been tediously slow. If the man could do what he promised he must be tolerated even if not actively liked.

'You are discourteous,' snapped Bassein. 'Ser Prome is our guest. He has come to help us. He is worthy of respect.'

'My apologies.' Luang bowed, as much to hide his face as to show his deference. 'It is just that this waiting – ' He gestured beyond the dome. 'How much longer must we wait?'

The burly man had finished his testing. Now he sank strong teeth into a slab of the strongly flavored meat. A woman helped herself to a cake, another to a juicy fruit. Within seconds, it seemed, all were thronged around the tables.

'Not long,' said Bassein. 'They are relaxing. Once they have eaten they will reach for the wine.' He lifted his binoculars again. The burly man, he thought, surely would be the first. Or, perhaps, no. Already he had proved his caution. He could wait until others had drunk, watching, joining in only when he was convinced the wine was harmless. That woman, then? Or the man with the scarred cheek?

'Have your guards been alerted?' Ser Prome had not moved from where he stood behind the others. 'As I warned you, the results will be spectacular.'

'They have their orders.' Bassein spoke distantly, concentrating on the scene below. The man with the scarred cheek reached for a jug, tilted it, cautiously tasted. He grinned, pleased, and swallowed deeply. Too deeply, perhaps. Bassein said, 'Perhaps

6

we should have used something other than wine, If they become intoxicated – '

'If you followed my instructions the alcohol content is low,' interrupted Ser Prome. His face betrayed nothing of the impatient arrogance he felt for the two officers. As expected they were victims of their heritage, the seemingly overriding inability to wait in silence. And yet they could be used.

'Look at them!' Luang echoed his disgust. 'Eating and drinking like animals.'

Bassein said nothing, watching.

The scarred man reached for a jug of wine. Another lifted it before he could grip it and Bassein saw the disfigured face contort in anger. He said something and the man with the jug raised it and, without hesitation, smashed it down hard on the other's skull. The jug was heavy. Bone splintered in a gush of red and gray, blood and brains spurting among the broken pottery, the flood of wine.

'Now!' breathed Luang. 'It begins!'

Horror had replaced the idyllic scene. The sward with its bright flowers became the place of carnage. Men, women, mouths open in screams, faces ugly with maniacal rage, threw themselves one against the other. Jugs shattered to provide crude weapons, savage points ripping at throats and eyes, blood staining the ground. A man kicked another in the groin, kicked again as he fell, his boot turning a face into a mass of red and oozing pulp. A woman sprang at him, fingers ripping at his eyes. Blinded, he turned to trip over a table, to fall rolling among the scattered food, rising to fall again, to twitch among threshing legs, to drown in his own blood as a heel crushed his throat.

There was no sound and Bassein was glad of it. He could imagine the screams, the shouts, the shrieks of agony.

In a few minutes what had appeared to be a harmless picnic had turned into a ghastly shambles. A hundred men and women fighting, killing, being killed in turn. Through the binoculars he could see their faces, distorted, filled with naked hate, burning with the fury of savage blood-lust. Safe as he was here in the observation dome, with armed guards between the tripod and those in the valley, he felt a sudden terror. If they should attack, somehow overcome the guards, reach this place –

'The guards!' snapped Luang. 'Quickly!'

A knot of survivors, numbering about a dozen, were running

7

toward the ring of trees. Another headed for the lake, slipping on the edge, fighting even as they drowned. Swans made shadows on the grass as they took to wing.

Bassein shook himself. Once, on Dihun, he had attended the arena and watched as men fought and died, but that had been nothing like this. There he had felt a rising euphoria, gaining a vicarious pleasure at watching wounds and blood and impersonal death. Now he felt only a sickness as he watched men turn into beasts.

'The guards,' said Luang again. 'With your permission, Marshal?'

Bassein nodded, unable to tear his eyes away from the carnage below. Luang stepped to a communicator and rapped a quick order. The waiting guards advanced from the ring of trees.

They were blank-faced men, disciplined, accustomed to obey without question. From their rifles spat a stream of fire, the self-propelled missiles venting their energy in gouts of flame as they struck. Bodies ripped open spilling intestines, heads vanished from shoulders, limbs fell to litter the bloodstained ground.

'All of them,' said the Chambodian flatly. 'They must all be destroyed.'

Luang relayed the order, watching as the guards moved across the valley, firing at every figure whether dead or alive.

'The guards also should be eliminated,' said the tall alien. 'The need for secrecy is paramount.'

'No.' Bassein drew a deep breath. Shooting at the dead, the maimed, and the living was bad enough, but they were criminals and expendable. 'There is no need.'

'They may talk.'

'About what? An experiment which failed. Those chosen to be rehabilitated suddenly rebelled and tried to make a break. They began to fight among themselves and then turned on the guards. The action was justified.'

'Weakness,' said the Chambodian. 'An attribute of your race. I am not surprised that Merah has for so long suffered beneath the Terran heel. Even when I show you how that dominance can be negated, still you hesitate. Well, the decision is yours.'

Watching the face of the marshal he wondered if perhaps he had gone a little too far. Even the monkeymen had their pride. Then he saw Luang's expression and knew that he had made no

8

mistake. The younger man was impatient for glory. Eager to accept the help he offered and not thinking or perhaps not caring about the risk he and his world would run.

'Perhaps, Marshal, we should do as Ser Prome suggests?'

'No!' Bassein was definite. 'We are a civilized people, not barbarians. Those guards are loyal; I will not repay that loyalty with death. And there is no need. As I said, the action can be explained and justified. It could even be used to combat those liberals who constantly demand penal reform. A proof that intransigents cannot be trusted.'

'As you wish, Marshal.'

As I wish, thought Bassein bleakly. But for how long? Already the signs of impatience were clear. Luang, his closest aide, a man whom he had lifted to high position, and he too was restless. And there were others in the military junta, restrained until now by the futility of combating Terran Control. Yet a world dedicated to a military system had to expand or perish. Sandwiched as they were between the Terran Sphere and the Chambodian Complex a decision had to be made. Terra offered peace and protection, Chambodia the same, yet how could a world of men fit into an alien complex?

He said, quietly, 'This discovery of yours, Ser Prome. Have others the knowledge you possess?'

'No.'

'Then how can you be sure we won't turn it against your own people?'

'You cannot. Turn it against us, I mean. We are too dissimilar as regards our metabolism and cortical development. But, Marshal, with respect, all this has been explained.'

More than once and in greater detail; there had been experiments too, but nothing like this. Bassein turned from the window, unwilling to stare at the bodies below. They would be collected and disposed of, but would he ever forget?

'I will be frank,' said the alien. 'With my help you can achieve greatness. I have shown you how. In return you will sign a treaty with the Chambodian Complex. You will also give me the facilities I requested for my research together with land and money. A small exchange, I think, for what you can achieve. Total independence, the forming of a new empire, Merah as the center of a viable culture. Once Terra has been weakened your

9

forces can move in. A dozen habitable worlds, more, and all accepting your domination.'

Tempting bait to offer ambitious men. Iressistible to a world already straining its economy and faced with internal disquiet. And Bassein knew that if he refused others would not. Luang for one. And there were other worlds just as ambitious with men just as dedicated. A trap, he thought bleakly, but the jaws had already closed. Like it or not he had no choice but to agree.

CHAPTER TWO

She was small with a pert face and sparkling blue eyes, and neatly dressed in a uniform of green, the crest of Terran Control stitched on her left shoulder. Her name was Susan Wells and, for a full lieutenant, she seemed rather young.

'Just one last test, Cap.' She smiled. 'And then we'll let you go.'

Kennedy relaxed gratefully in the chair. He was nude but for shorts, electrodes fastened to various parts of his body, more festooning his scalp. Idly he watched as the girl threw switches and studied dials. Her attention was casual, the real work was being done by the medical computer, but she was very conscious of the way she filled her unform, conscious too of the importance of the man undergoing routine examination.

Not every day did she get the chance to order around a member of FATE.

'Well,' he said after a few minutes. 'Do I pass?'

'I'm afraid so. No retirement for you yet and no excuse for keeping you around. Physically you're perfect. A classic example of a treble A-One.'

'And mentally?'

'The same.' She glanced down at the computer's findings as they emerged on a paper roll from the readout. 'Just as I thought. No deterioration of any kind. Fast reflexes, quick mental agility even while under stress, strong emotional control, no sign of any disorientation, high concentration index, high degree of intuition, high empathy level, high – damn it, Cap! Why do you have to be so good?'

They both knew the answer. The need too for routine examination. Any man given the literal power of life and death had to be in peak condition. Like all Free Acting Terran Envoys Kennedy could act as judge, jury, and executioner, summon

11

the power to destroy a world, take whatever steps he saw fit to resolve any situation threatening the peace of the Terran Sphere.

'The trouble is that you're too damn good,' she grumbled as she removed the electrodes. 'You make all the men around here seem pretty small fry in comparison. Have you a brother?'

'No.'

'A pity. If you had one and he was here on Earth I'd look him up. By the time you come back for another routine check I'll be gone.'

'Up or out?'

'Both, I hope. A promotion to Verne. Have you ever been there?'

'Third world of Sirius?' Kennedy nodded. 'You'll like it there. Plenty of water if you like to sail or swim, mountains if you want to climb, and the gliding is superb.'

'Sports,' she snorted. 'How about the social life?'

'Well, now,' he said, studying her. 'In my opinion you'll land a minor official in a week. A local governor might take a little longer, say ten days. Of course, if you want to marry the Principal that might take a month – if his wife doesn't get to you first.'

'Flattery will get you anywhere,' she said, pleased. 'All right, you can go now. Don't forget the reception tonight. Orders from on high. Refuse and the Director will have your head on a plate.'

Knowing Elias Weyburn, Kennedy could well believe it.

Dressed, he paused in the street. It was good to be back on Earth. No other planet had quite the same feel or atmosphere and, now that the bad old days were gone, Terra was a paradise indeed. Soaring buildings held the teeming population, graceful edifices which ornamented the sky, the towers interspersed with wide parks and recreational areas. Beyond lay rolling farms and industrial complexes, the whole joined by a network of transportation systems. The air was brisk and clean, atomic power had taken care of pollution, and stellar expansion had made degrading poverty a thing of the past.

With time to kill he wandered the city. The *Mordain* was in for overhaul, Penza Saratov refusing to leave his beloved engines and keeping a sharp eye on the technicians, much to their disgust. Chemile had been adopted by an artistic group and was giving a series of lectures and demonstrations. Professor Jarl Luden had vanished into the depths of the Metropolitan Museum to mull over ancient scrolls and artifacts. But, in Greater New York, it was no discomfort to be alone.

Kennedy watched a troupe of Boddari dancers, ate a selective meal in a rotating restaurant, enjoyed a vapor bath, and spent a while swimming in an offshore lagoon stocked with dolphins and sportive mermaids. The dolphins could be ridden; the mermaids, skilled aquarists, vied with each other for his company. As night fell he remembered the command.

The party was in full swing when he arrived. Kennedy stood at the door of the main hall looking at the assembled guests, a scatter of minor diplomats and others who were not so minor from a hundred worlds: people of Earth and worlds affiliated under the Terran Sphere; colorful figures from adjoining sectors: Deltanians, Lartustians, those from Altanis, some from Ragan. All friends of Terra or, at least, members of combines which were not at actual war. The difference, he knew, was small, but important.

'Cap!' Carl Justine, young, fresh-faced, a minor diplomat in Terran Control, came toward him, hand extended. 'Man, it's good to see you!'

'And you.' Their hands touched, pressed. Kennedy liked Justine; they had known each other years ago before various duties had driven them apart. 'What's all this for? Just common goodwill or is there something deep going on?'

'Just oil to ease the tension.' Justine lifted his glass. 'A chance for old friends to meet and old enemies to heal wounds. You know how it is. The art of diplomacy is getting your adversary well and truly stoned and then picking the gold from his fillings. At least that's what my grandfather used to say. No gold now, of course, and no fillings, not with regrafts, but the principle's the same.'

'Your grandfather,' said Kennedy dryly, 'must have had a long memory.'

'He did. And his grandfather before him. All diplomats. I'm the last of an unbroken line of professional liars.' Justine shrugged. 'Well, it's a living. Not that I'd rather be out there with you, but space is no place for a man with a family.' He glanced over the hall. Couples were dancing to the music from a living band, the players dressed in the fashion of a bygone age. Waiters, similarly dressed, moved among the guests with trays

13

of snacks and drinks. Justine summoned one, selected a glass which he handed to Kennedy. 'Get that down you while I move around. If you need an introduction, just yell.'

Kennedy nodded, sipped at the drink, then set down the glass as two girls came toward him. Both were young, dressed in a shimmer of luminescent scales, eyes and lips thick with cosmetics.

One said, 'You're mine. I saw you first. Tell this interloper to go away.'

'Like hell,' said her companion brusquely. 'Steal him and you'll meet me tomorrow in the gymnasium.'

'Peace,' said Kennedy. 'You're too young and pretty to fight. In any case I'm spoken for.'

He quickly moved away before they could argue, heading toward the high windows at the end of which stood a cluster of men, one of whom he recognized. Director Elias Weyburn had been likened to a brooding eagle, but Kennedy always thought of him as a slumberous dog. A big one, less the traditional barrel of brandy but with the sharp teeth and big ears still intact. Now his heavy face was somber, his eyes, pouched and lined, peering from beneath heavy brows.

He looked at Kennedy, stared past him, ignoring him as he concentrated on what others of the group were saying.

'I had always understood that Terra was a haven of peace,' said a tall, hard-faced man. Serge Helbroft, ambassador of the Altanian Oligarchy. 'And yet what do I find? Groups of young people parading at the edge of the spaceport with banners and chanting slogans. The police dispersed them, of course, but how can such things be here on Earth?'

'You will see much of this on Terra.' Cran Thorm, wearing the traditional garb of Ragan, made no secret of his contempt. 'The Terran Sphere, despite its pious claims, does not encourage the free expression of the individual.'

'On the contrary,' said Weyburn acidly. 'However, the demonstration you speak of was not authorized by the police. The spacefield is no place to stage a protest at the treatment of another world's disaffected. Your reputation, Ambassador, had preceded you.'

'Meaning?'

'Nothing personal, I am certain. However, your government is not noted for its gentle treatment of those who disagree with its policies. The young people you speak of acted unwisely; but since when have children ever been wise?'

'On Ragan we know how to deal with such things.'

'True,' admitted Weyburn mildly. 'And on Altan also, no doubt. With steel and fire and irritant gases. However, that is your concern. Terran Control is not interested in how you manage your own worlds.'

'Any violation of our autonomy by any power will be dealt with as deserved,' snapped Serge Helbroft. 'We are not children to run to our mother at the slightest injury.'

Cran Thorm echoed the sentiment, adding, 'As far as I can see such demonstrations are a sure sign of decadence. It could be that Terra is losing its grip and should think of taking a lesser place in the Galaxy.'

The old song, thought Weyburn grimly. Bellicose worlds chafing at the slightest hint of criticism or restraint. Eager and avid to step in and take over more civilized planets. But never Earth, he promised himself bleakly. Never any planet in the Terran Sphere. Not while the MALACAs stood ready to strike with fire and destruction any who stepped too far out of line. And not when FATE could cut down any rancid weed which threatened to poison the air of peaceful worlds.

His glass was empty. He took another, glancing at Kennedy where he stood to one side, chatting to a Merahinian. He had deliberately ignored the man, trusting to Cap's intelligence to know that it was intentional. The less these strutting fools knew of his associates the better; but while Cap was on Earth it was better that he should see them. Later they would talk.

The group dissolved, splintering to form new combinations. The music grew a trifle louder, the talk a little higher as good food and drink loosened tongues and eased tensions. Kennedy watched, listened, dodged the attentions of daughters and wives who should have known better but who seemed to regard him as fair game. To those who asked he admitted that he was a businessman hoping to make a few useful contacts. To those who probed more deeply he confessed that he was unmarried. In three hours he had been given enough invitations to private dinners to have lasted a couple of years.

Bored, he danced a little, drank even less. He had no love for formal receptions and wouldn't have come had not Weyburn made it an order. And the Director would not have done that

15

without a reason. Despite his boredom Kennedy remained alert.

Justine came toward him at the same time as a girl carrying a glass in each hand. They collided, Justine spilling his own drink. Laughing, he took one from the girl's hand.

'You don't need them both, my dear.'

'But – ' She broke off, looking at Kennedy. 'I was – never mind.'

'I spoiled her evening.' Justine lifted the glass he had taken in a silent toast to her departing back. 'She wanted to get into conversation with you and I ruined the attempt. Never mind. She'll be back.' He sipped and swallowed the contents of the glass. He'd had, thought Kennedy, a little too much already.

Justine shook his head when he hinted as much.

'No, Cap. In my job you get used to it. It might look as if I'm guzzling, but that's just for appearances. In fact, this is the third whole drink of the evening. The first with you, the second with the ambassador, and now this. All the rest were sipped and put aside.' He scowled around the hall. 'Doesn't this get you? Damn it, Cap, you'll never know how much I envy you. If things had been different – ' He broke off, shrugging. 'Well, there it is. Some pass the tests; others don't. I was one of the unlucky ones.'

Kennedy said, 'You've compensations.'

'My family? You're right, but at times – ' He broke off again. 'I don't know what's getting into me. Forget it.'

'Maybe you should go home.'

'Quit the party? Hell, why not? Be seeing you, Cap.'

Outside, it was almost dawn. Justine stood on the steps, scowling, then moved down toward a waiting cab.

'Home,' he said, and gave the address.

His house was on the edge of the city, one of a row which had been built back in the old days when remembered troubles had made men seek protection as well as comfort. As the cab came to a halt, he threw the driver money and stalked to the door. A light glowed as the identification plate checked his pattern against that stored in its memory, winking out as the panel slid aside.

Inside, a wide staircase led from the hall into the upper regions. Soft carpets covered the floor and pedestals held delicate objects of art, vases, statuettes, bowls, and other items of value culled from a hundred worlds. He stepped to where a

16

fragment of pottery stood beneath a soft light, a relic of a dynasty of the ancient past. Deliberately he picked it up, dropped it, smashing aeons of loving care beneath his heel.

'Carl!' A voice from above, feminine, cultured. 'Carl! Is that you?'

He ignored it, going across the hall to where a door of paneled wood stood sunken into the wall. Lights glowed beyond as he opened it, revealing a long chamber lined with books and hung with a wide assortment of trophies. The heads of animals, stuffed and mounted, stared down with glassy eyes. Horned, spined, wreathed with spikes. The gaping mandibles of a giant insect gaped with impotent fury. A sea-creature spread hooked tendrils over the ceiling. The inheritance he had gained from sportive ancestors as were the weapons glinting on the walls. Rifles, shotguns, lasers, Diones, muskets, crossbows, swords, spears, and other fabrications of edged and pointed metal all neatly set, their metal bright, edges sharp.

Justine roved among them, touching, caressing, his eyes distant and then, as the voice called again from above, he reached a decision. From the primitive display he selected a machete of dull iron and stood for a moment swinging the heavy weapon. Then, quickly, he ran from the room and up the stairs beyond.

2

CHAPTER THREE

Jud Harbin put down the report and stared bleakly before him. His face was harsh, craggy, engraved with lines of rigid determination, a mask behind which the Supremo of Terran military power marshaled his thoughts; but this had hit him hard.

'Justine,' he said. 'It doesn't seem possible.'

'It's true enough.' Weyburn had seen enough of the seamy side of life to remain detached. 'His wife, his two children, his mother-in-law, his uncle. He damned near chopped them to mincemeat. The house signaled for help when he started a fire. The thermo-couples gave the location, but there was little the firemen could do. The place was as tough as a stronghold. It took them the best part of an hour to get inside.'

'And Justine?'

'Dead. The house was self-protecting. It sealed the room where the fire was and dumped foam. Justine was cold when they found him. Anoxemia.'

Harbin made no comment.

'It was probably for the best,' said Conrad Weit after a moment. 'He wouldn't have wanted to live knowing what he had done.'

'Maybe not.' Weyburn was curt. Justine had worked for the Head of Diplomacy and Weit would have a personal interest, but the Director had no time for sentiment. 'But he might have been able to tell us why he did it. You were one of the last to see him alive, Cap. Have you any ideas?'

Kennedy shook his head. Weyburn had invited him to the conference and he had a pretty good idea why. When high officials died in suspicious circumstances the odor of assassination was always present. And yet, in this case, it was hard to see how anyone else could have been responsible. Justine had died alone in a locked house and by his own hand.

He said, 'Carl seemed a little detached, but that was all.'

'Just that?'

'Yes,' said Kennedy. 'We were talking about his family and he decided to go home. The last I saw of him he was walking toward the doors.'

Another blank wall, thought Weyburn, and then was angry at himself for the quick surrender. It couldn't be left at that; he would be failing in his duty if he even considered that it could. *I'm tired,* he thought, but it wasn't just physical fatigue which bunched his muscles into aching protest. In this underground room he and Harbin and Weit had pondered the destinies of worlds. From the broad aspects of political policy down to the most minute detail of positive action. Planning, always planning, scheme after scheme, endless hours spent in ensuring the peace of the Terran Sphere. Eternal vigilance, he reminded himself, was the price of liberty. He could understand why some considered the price to be too high.

And now this.

Looking at Weit, he said, 'You were his boss. He worked for your department and you were pretty close. Have you any suggestions?'

'No. Justine, on the face of it, was a well-adjusted individual with everything to live for. He had money, good health, an attractive wife, an assured career – ' He broke off, making a helpless gesture. 'What makes a man do a thing like that? He must have gone insane.'

Weyburn raised his eyebrows. 'Jud?'

'I don't know.' Harbin shrugged. 'I suppose it's barely possible.'

'Cap?'

'Without evidence it's hard to be sure,' said Kennedy thoughtfully. 'I used to know Carl pretty well in the old days and I would have said that he was about as stable as a man could be. But a man can change. Even so I would never have considered him to be a pathological homicide. Suicide, maybe, but why take his family with him? Have there been other similar incidents?'

'You've hit it, Cap,' said Weyburn. 'There have. And that's why I don't think insanity is the answer. It can't be. Once, yes. Twice, yes. Three times, maybe. Coincidences happen. But during the past three weeks we've had fifteen similar cases. Men, for no apparent reason, suddenly going berserk. Killing their wives, their children, themselves. No one famous,' he added. 'No one in the public eye. Junior clerks, tradesmen, service engineers. All within the city. I think this Justine business is tied in with it.'

'He went insane,' said Weit. 'It's the only logical explanation.'

Weyburn shrugged. 'Maybe, but right or wrong it's the rumor we're going to spread around. Justine just went crazy – so we can forget all about him. Only it isn't the answer and we all know it. A man like Justine doesn't reach high office without being checked, and he showed no trace of mental instability. His last examination was two days ago and checked out double A-One. And he had no special duties until last night.'

'The reception,' said Weit. 'Justine took my place as official host.'

'I've had men checking,' continued Weyburn. 'Justine left the party about dawn. He didn't tell anyone he was leaving aside from Cap. He took a cab and had himself driven straight home. The journey took about an hour. He must have started his butchery immediately.'

He caught the expression on Weit's face, the distaste on Harbin's, and mentally shrugged. Harbin dealt in big, bright, and shining things and fought his battles in the open. Weit was used to the elaborate courtesy of diplomatic maneuvering and fought his wars with words. The Director of Terran Control worked in the dark and could not afford to be squeamish.

'All right,' he said. 'Let's look at what we've got. A man with apparently everything to live for suddenly blows his top. He abandons his duties, rushes home, kills his family and tries to destroy his house. He dies trying.' He leaned back, pouched eyes and sagging jowls giving him a deceptively somnolent appearance. 'If we rule out insanity, what have we got left?'

'Muder,' said Kennedy.

'Right, Cap.' Weyburn leaned forward and slammed his hand on the table. 'No matter what it looks like that's all it can be. Let's check it out.'

Mai Alexandovich was a tall, pale man with stooped shoulders and a weak mouth and chin, but there was nothing feeble about his mind. As a pathologist and acting psychiatrist he was high in his profession. He met Kennedy and Weyburn in the privacy of his office and he was positive as to his findings.

20

'Your suspicions are correct,' he said. 'It was undoubtedly murder.'

'You are sure of that?' Weyburn was insistent.

'I am. A man does not go suddenly insane just like that.' Alexandovich snapped his fingers. 'Not even when there is extreme and excessive emotional, physical, and mental pressure. In such a case a man might be thrown into panic, suffer a total disorientation, be the victim of hallucinations of various kinds, and even appear, to a layman, to be insane. But that would be a wrong definition. In any case Justine was not subjected to such pressures. His life was one of normal routine. For such a man to lose his mental stability there must always be a preliminary period of emotional disturbance, a breaking or straining of the usual living-pattern. Justine displayed no sign of any such symptoms.'

Weyburn snapped, 'There can be no doubt of that?'

'None. I have carefully examined the computer records.'

'So he was got at,' said Kennedy. 'But how?'

'And why?' The question troubled Weyburn. 'What did the autopsy show?'

'Nothing unexpected,' said Alexandovich. 'The man died because of lack of oxygen. His lungs were full of smoke and the entire endocrine balance was in a state compatible to extreme tension and nervous stimulation. The stomach held food, alcohol, traces of exotic spices, chemical flavorings, artificial colorings – what was to be expected as he had been to a party, but nothing of a harmful or toxic nature. The blood, naturally, held a high density of adrenaline which shows that he must have been in an extremity of rage or fear.'

'Fear strong enough to have paralyzed his vocal cords?'

Alexandovich shrugged. 'Perhaps, Director. It is impossible to say. Why do you ask?'

'Justine didn't have to die. He could have escaped from the sealed room had he wished. The house-controls had a sonic key and could be overridden by a shouted command.' Weyburn pursed his lips. 'Could he shout? Was there anything wrong with his throat?'

'Not that I could discover. Naturally, I have been looking for evidence of the use of some form of nerve poison, but without success. From the record of his movements we can eliminate the possibility of hypnotic conditioning. He was not so conditioned when examined, and every moment of his time has been accounted for since. The testimony of the cabdriver shows that he did not stop on the way. I assume the man can be believed?'

Weyburn nodded.

'The brief lapse of time between his arrival home and the commencement of the slaughter shows that the latter may have been premeditated. Possibly that is why he left the reception so hurriedly. The violence of the attack shows that it must have stemmed from a maniacal rage. Rage which passed the border of sane behavior in its frenzied application and which later may have been transmuted to fear. I am inclined to believe that it did not. The pattern of destruction is too classical for that.'

'A textbook example of a man bent on self-destruction,' said Kennedy thoughtfully. 'He wanted not only to destroy himself, but every extension of his being. His wife, his relatives, his children, even his house. Everything.'

'Exactly.' Alexandovich was impressed. 'I see that you understand these matters.'

As a master of psychology that wasn't surprising, but Kennedy didn't explain.

Weyburn said, 'So it was suicide. But you called it murder. Why?'

Alexandovich looked surprised. 'It is surely obvious. His attack of insanity could not have been normal. It is obvious that Justine must have been the victim of some external influence. Whoever provided that influence was guilty of the resultant deaths. That is why I call it murder.'

'This outside influence,' said Weyburn. 'Could it have been a drug of some kind?'

'I found no evidence of any suspicious substance.

'Which doesn't mean that none exists,' said Kennedy. 'Assume that it does. How would it need to work to force a man like Justine to do what he did?'

Alexandovich hesitated. 'I do not care to speculate. Even deep and sustained hypnosis would be an extremely unreliable instrument to achieve such an end, and we know that hypnosis was not used.'

'We're treading old ground,' snapped Weyburn. 'What we need here is imagination. Cap! Tell him how it could be done!'

'Justine was dissatisfied,' said Kennedy. 'He hid it well, but with me he opened up a little. He was bored and regretted not having passed the tests which would have given him a more adventurous life. His house was full of trophies and weapons, relics of his forebears who had done what he hadn't. It must have added to his resentment. We know little of his personal life; there could have been marital strain. He was also supporting his relatives. They could have been a little overbearing.'

Alexandovich frowned. 'So?'

'Meeting me accentuated his feeling of inadequacy and, because it is a psychological fact that a man will never blame himself for what he is, but always find external excuses, he would have felt anger at those he considered to be the cause of his personal failure. Now, suppose that while he was in that exact mental and emotional situation, something was given to him which nullified the censor. What, in your professional opinion, would happen?'

'No barriers,' said Alexandovich. He was shaken. 'No check between subconscious desire and conscious control. Nothing to prevent the execution of every intention.'

'And?'

'He would kill. He would destroy everything he blamed for his personal failure. In a sense he would be taking revenge on life itself. And his own death would be inevitable.'

It was a vicious weapon and one against which there could be no defense. The savage primitive remained in everyone no matter how sophisticated the culture. The painfully acquired veneer of civilization was too fragile to combat the urgings of the subconscious without the aid of the censor.

Weyburn said, 'Cap. Those other cases?'

'Tests to determine the efficiency of the drug. Perhaps to discover the relationship between dosage and time of taking effect. If traces could not be found it must be rapidly absorbed and quick to act. Which means that whatever was given to Justine had to be delivered at the reception.'

'One thousand three hundred and twenty-eight official guests,' said Weyburn grimly. 'Not counting the staff. They'll all have to be checked, Cap. Someone had a reason for fixing Justine and we've got to find out who.'

CHAPTER FOUR

Professor Jarl Luden was at peace. Sitting at a table deep beneath the structure of the Metropolitan Museum, surrounded by moldering tomes and records of ancient artifacts, he was as contented as a man could be. To the assistant who brought new records and quietly supplied cups of coffee, he was something of a novelty. His thin body and grave features surmounted by thick gray hair swept back from a high forehead bespoke the dedicated scholar, but his garish clothing, the high-collared blouse, the flared pants, and brilliant sash belonged to a dilettante. A weakness, she thought. An eccentricity to compensate, perhaps, for an unadventurous life. She didn't know the professor.

He turned a page, carefully made a notation on the pad at his side, reached for another volume. Here, in the lower levels, it was very quiet; only a scatter of privileged scholars were allowed access to the original works. Kennedy's boots made a dull thudding as he stepped toward the table.

'Cap!' Luden smiled, his thin lips curving to reveal his pleasure. 'A most unexpected pleasure. You have arrived at a propitious moment. I have just discovered a most interesting item in an old Egyptian scroll. It deals with magical rituals associated with the interment of the dead and there is a close affinity to the ceremonies of the Heldara tribe on Alpha Centauri Three. It could be a sheer coincidence, of course, but I am inclined to believe that it is more than that. Also, on an Incan temple, there is what can only be a depiction of the Zheltyana Sign. I must make cross-references, naturally, and if possible visit the site for a personal inspection, but the implications are entrancing.'

'Sorry, Jarl, but personal inspections will have to wait.'

'Trouble, Cap?' Luden pursed his lips as Kennedy related

24

what had happened. 'Your conclusions, of course, have yet to be verified, but from the evidence I would say that you are correct. In which case the situation gives rise to concern.'

Kennedy said, dryly, 'Yes, Jarl. I think it is safe to say that.'

As always Luden was veering to the side of caution, but the understatement deserved a prize. In the eternal game of push and counterpush, with shifting balances of power, of hungry worlds eager to snatch undeserved rewards and envious races hating the tranquillity established by the *Pax Terra*, Earth was a prime target. If its leaders could be turned insane. If terror could be slipped into the drinking water so that entire cities exploded into savage violence and the economic and industrial structure be weakened and destroyed, the vultures would move in.

'We've no time to waste, Jarl.' Kennedy kept his voice low, a blurred susurration which could not be heard a few feet from where they sat. 'I want you to do some checking. First the laboratories of Dr Wuhun on Taipan. He has done work on the surgical elimination of the censor using dogs and rats. Then the clinic at Lusanne. Madam Chee is using drug therapy based on a similar pattern. Find out if there have been any sudden resignations of staff connected with research or practice. Also, if there have been any alien visitors showing an unusual interest.'

'Chambodians, Cap?'

'Especially Chambodians, but I doubt if they would have made a personal appearance. Their interest would have been hard to justify. Get hold of Veem. He may be able to help you.'

'He won't like it, Cap. You know how Veem is. At the moment he's enjoying himself with all those lectures and doting females.'

'He'll do it,' said Kennedy. 'If not he can wait at the *Mordain* with Penza.'

'And he'll like that even less,' said Luden. 'Penza will get him cleaning and checking, and Veem hates routine.' He sighed as he looked at the stacks of ancient records. 'A pity,' he murmured. 'A few more days and I may have made a fresh discovery. There is a basis of truth in the old legends, Cap. Many of the old religions make it plain that early space travelers must have landed on Earth and contacted the natives. They could have brought information on the Zheltyana, or the Ancient Race may even have made a personal appearance. Long before recorded history, of course, far before the time when men were developed from primitive life-forms. Perhaps they could have had something to do with the disappearance of the reptiles.'

'Perhaps,' said Kennedy. 'Maybe, one day, we'll find out.'

But not today, not when there were more urgent problems to be solved.

He said, as Luden rose from the table, 'Don't feel too bad about it, Jarl. The records have waited for thousands of years. They'll still be here when you want to study them again.'

'True,' admitted Luden. He carefully pocketed his notations. They could be studied at leisure when on flight in the *Mordain*. It would take a lifetime to make a thorough search, that and the use of a large computer to assemble all available data, but he would do what he could. 'How shall I contact you, Cap?'

'Through Weyburn. I'm going to see what the computer has discovered about the party.'

The giant computers of Terran Control were housed five hundred feet below a public library. It was a convenient location – the library was open twenty-four hours a day and the comings and goings of those who visited it were lost in the crowd.

Kennedy swung through the main entrance and paused to see if he had been followed. A man wearing purple and maroon passed him without a glance. Another, more soberly dressed, hesitated for a fraction before moving on to study a map of the city. Kennedy watched him, noting the shape of his head, the slope of his shoulders, things impossible to disguise. The face was nondescript, a collection of features over which the eye passed without catching anything to hold the attention: A casual wanderer, perhaps, killing time; a tourist or someone waiting for a companion. It was unlikely that he had been followed, but Kennedy took nothing for granted.

He waited five minutes, then swung through the racks of reading matter, past the general reference section, and into a room fitted out as a lecture hall. Half the seats were filled, faces limned in the shadows by the light streaming from one wall as a series of slides illustrated the life-cycle of the liver fluke. A door opened on a narrow passage, another to a row of toilets reserved for the use of staff. Kennedy entered the third cubicle from the end, closed the door and rested the palm of his hand against a tile. Electronic devices scanned his body and, abruptly, the floor opened beneath his feet, depositing him into a shaft which led him to the regions below.

Hilda Thorenson was the technician in charge of the Justine operation. A tall, nordic goddess, she leaned back in her chair, face marked with the lines of fatigue. Her eyes were closed. She opened them as Kennedy halted at her desk.

'I've been expecting you,' she said. 'Weyburn told me to deal direct. You want some coffee?'

'You have some,' he said. 'You look as if you could use it.'

'You're right there, Cap,' she said gratefully. 'It's been a long haul.' Cup in hand, she gestured at the graphs littering her desk. 'Well, here it is . . . Working on the basis that something was given to Justine during the party, we feel it would most logically have been given in a drink. The probability for that is over ninety percent. That rules out the waiters; the risk of Justine taking the wrong glass or of not taking one at all was too great. Anyway, we checked out the staff. Negative.'

Kennedy didn't ask how they had been checked. Terran Control had its own methods.

'Then we looked for associated modes of conduct and cross-checked on what we found,' continued the woman. 'You know, someone saw someone else give someone a drink and then someone saw who saw the someone – ' She broke off, irritated. 'I guess I must be tired. What I really mean is that we checked alibis. All of them.'

With over a thousand guests and a large staff it meant thousands of assorted bits of data to be fed into the machine, there to be processed and collated. No wonder the woman was tired.

'Finally we came up with this.' Her finger made tapping motions as she explained the graph spread before them. 'This was compiled from the testimony of witnesses, cross-checked by the computer, and positioned in time and space. It is a portion of the main hall close to the main doors. These dots are people, Justine, Serge Helbroft, Cran Thorm, Ahun Zemao – '

'A Merahinian?'

'Yes. The only one present. The member of a trade delegation interested in buying machine tools and instructional tapes of vacuum-form processing. You note they are all in fairly close proximity.'

Kennedy nodded. 'And the other dots?'

'Substantive witnesses who don't enter the action. As we don't know the exact time between Justine taking the stuff and its taking effect we have to guess. We can assume that it was fairly short; I have allowed a fifty percent margin of maximum probability.'

'Justine said something about having three drinks,' said Kennedy. 'The second was with the ambassador. That would have been Serge Helbroft.'

'Exactly. Now follow this. A waiter handed around drinks. Justine took one and then passed it to the Merahinian. Helbroft took another and passed it to Justine. He could have slipped something into it, but I don't think so. The time was too early. Now look at this. She reached for another sheet. 'You're in this one, Cap. The time is just before dawn. Can you remember exactly what happened?'

Kennedy had good recall. He said, 'There was a girl. She came toward us carrying a couple of drinks. Justine took one and drank it.'

'Yes,' she said. 'But it wasn't just like that, was it?'

'No,' he admitted. 'Justine bumped into her and spilled the drink he was carrying. He took one which she was holding and which she – '

'That's right.' Hilda Thorenson leaned back, her face grim. 'The drink she intended to pass to you. The incident was seen by a waiter. It's pretty obvious that Justine got it by accident – that he was never intended to be the victim at all. You were, Cap. That poison was aimed at you.'

Kennedy said nothing, thinking, remembering. The girl had been tall, willowy, attractive in a sheer gown. Her face? He frowned, concentrating. 'Deep blue eyes,' he said. 'A full lower lip. Hair light brown and cut so as to form a helmet over her skull. Her shoulders sloped and her chin was marked by a slight cleft. High cheekbones and small lobes on her ears. Skin olive as if she had been sunbathing or was the resident of a semitropical zone. She had a mole on her left cheek and wore no rings.'

Interested, she said, 'Anything else?'

'She could have been a dancer and may have trained as a singer. Her voice held a low modulation.'

'Very good.' Hilda Thorenson was impressed. 'Considering that you only saw her for a moment and had no reason to give her special attention. Have you any idea of her height and weight? With that the computer should be able to dig up a name.'

He gave the information, waited as she operated a switch panel. Before she had finished her coffee the answer came.

'You were right,' she said, studying the readout. 'She has danced and sung in public. Two years ago she went on a tour to the Deltainian Sector. No criminal record. No medical history. Solvent, but has expensive tastes and her credit rating is touching the red. Unmarried, lives alone, at present a student of extraterrestrial art. Has worked as a receptionist, done some modeling, published a book of poems. Abstract stuff which were a commercial loss. She was born in Mekness of mixed parentage. The mole could be removed but was retained for reasons of cosmetic attraction.'

'Name?'

'Silmar Hayshan. She lives in the Stellar Tower in lower Manhattan.' She blinked as he reached over and took the slip from her hand. 'What are you going to do, Cap?'

'Find her,' he said flatly. 'Talk to her. If she wanted to kill me I'd like to know why.'

The Stellar Tower reared for a thousand feet from a surround of grass dotted with fountains and beds of brilliant flowers. Silmar Hayshan lived on the fifty-eighth floor and was apparently not at home. Kennedy rang three times, then stooped to examine the lock. It was a simple device and yielded beneath his trained hands. Inside he paused, looking at the main room of the apartment.

The floor was covered with rugs, abstract paintings on the walls, a deep couch facing a television screen, a record player to one side. A wide balcony lay beyond closed windows, flowers growing in pots, vines trained to frame the panes with riotous growth. It was a comfortable room and one betraying good taste and the wealth to pander to it. The air smelled stale and held a subtle acrid taint which caused him to frown.

Softly he called, 'Silmar Hayshan? Are you at home?'

He received no answer and had expected none. A room lay to one side and he examined a neat kitchen, the shelves scantily stocked with cheap staples. The bathroom was dry; the tub cold to his hand. The remaining room, a bedroom, was in darkness.

He paused at the door, sniffing, then quickly crossed to the window and drew back the curtains. Turning, he examined the room.

A rug had been kicked and lay in untidy folds. A gown lay beneath a small table bearing a lamp, a small vision screen, a single flower in a vase. Ash lay beneath a small pot of hammered brass, the incense from which it had come burned totally away. A pair of mules lay in one corner, a robe in another. A coverlet of rumpled silk embroidered with scarlet dragons lay on the double bed. On it, facedown, lay the naked body of a girl.

She was, Kennedy knew, quite dead.

He stood looking at her for a long moment. The face was buried in the pillow, one arm lifted and curved above her hair, the other hanging limp at her side. He could see no blood or other sign of injury, but there was no doubting her condition. Eyes watchful, he stepped from the window toward the bed. The hair was as he remembered, the one ear he could see, the shoulders, and general build. Gently he leaned forward, careful not to touch the bed, and felt her arm. The flesh was cold, hard.

He lifted his hand and gripped her shoulder, gently pulling. The body turned a little, one cheek coming into view, and he saw the remembered mole. Beneath the body, almost invisible, something lay caught between the coverlet and her flesh.

Kennedy dropped, burying his face in his hands, body hugging the floor as fire and thunder roared from the bed. He felt the shock, the heat, acrid gases stinging his lungs. Something spattered about the room and he felt an ugly wetness on the backs of his hands. Rising, he staggered into the other room. Behind him the bed was burning, filling the place with acrid smoke, the roiling clouds holding the stench of charred flesh and bone.

CHAPTER FIVE

'Booby-trapped,' said Weyburn. 'You were damned lucky to get out alive. What saved you?'

They were in the shooting range of Terran Control, the only relaxation the Director allowed himself, and it was like him to combine business with pleasure.

'I saw something,' said Kennedy. 'It shouldn't have been there. And I was suspicious.'

The smell, the atmosphere of the apartment, the sense of caution which had more than once saved his life. He watched as the Director threw a switch. On the far wall a Chambodian sprang to life, running toward a distant horizon. Weyburn waited until the figure grew small in simulated distance, then fired. A red spot glowed on the back of the skull as a bell rang success.

'It was a pressure bomb,' he said. 'Had you turned over the body, it would have blown your head off. As it was, you ducked just in time. Well, so much for the girl.'

'I doubt if she could have told us much,' said Kennedy. 'Someone must have paid her to give me that drink. They could have given any reason. How did she get into the reception?'

'A forged ticket.'

'Provided by the person who hired her. Someone who had to be at the party. He would have had to spike the drink, give it to her, and aim her my way. We should be able to find him.'

'We have,' said Weyburn curtly. 'That woman, Hilda Thorenson, is pretty smart. She made a check after you'd left. As far as she can gather, the most likely suspect is Aihun Zemao.'

'The Merahinian?'

'That's right. And, of course, he has diplomatic immunity. We can't grill him, but, by God, he'll be watched every second from now on. He and every member of his trade delegation

31

from now until they leave Earth.' Weyburn handed Kennedy the pistol. 'Let me see what you can do.'

Kennedy waited until the target was at extreme range, then fired five times in quick succession. A red spot glowed on each arm and leg, another on the back of the head.

'Anything in the apartment?'

'Nothing but the usual junk. Some travel folders, a specimen of ardash blooms sealed in plastic, a vial of erghal perfume. Clothes, cheap food, books, recordings of tribal music, incense from Wen.'

'Erghal perfume,' said Kennedy thoughtfully. 'That comes from Merah.'

'Something on your mind, Cap?'

'It could have been a gift. A woman like that would have appreciated it.'

'You're thinking of Aihun Zemao, but he couldn't have planted the bomb. That was a local product.'

'He could have got it.'

'But not planted it,' insisted Weyburn. 'I've had men check. Not that it matters; things like that can be arranged.' He fired again, scowling as he missed. 'Merah. That's too close to the Chambodian Complex for comfort. Those damned vultures are always looking for trouble and trying to find others to do their dirty work.' He flung down the pistol. 'To hell with it. Let's go and see what the local agent has found.'

The report was brief but disquieting: The military cabal increasing production of weapons, an enlargement of conscription, petty regulations hampering trade. Straws in a familiar wind.

'Merah is up to something,' decided Weyburn. 'They're flexing their muscles and getting ready for action of some kind. It could have nothing to do with our problem, but we can't take chances.' He checked a map. 'I'll have Harbin move MALACA Nine as close as they can get, and Commander Avery is discreet.'

He was discreet enough and diplomatic enough to broadcast the fact that the planet had requested assistance from the Mobile Aid Laboratory And Construction Authority. Merah could not object to the near presence of ships and men, the forces which Earth kept in space and which could destroy a world. Forces which were ostensibly for peace, but could be used for war.

'The thing which worries me, Cap,' said Weyburn, 'is the

way they selected you as a target. It's safe to assume that the Chambodians know of the existence of FATE or, if they don't know, they must suspect. They'd be fools if they didn't. They must have an agent on Earth who would know how to find men to do his dirty work. Like using that girl,' he added. 'Like killing her. Like setting up that bomb so as to catch anyone who might come looking. But for them to aim at you could mean they know who and what you are.'

'A leak,' said Kennedy. It was always possible. Men were only human and open to temptation if the price was right. Despite all precautions it was a perpetual problem.

A lamp flashed red on Weyburn's desk. As the Director threw a switch a man's face appeared on the screen.

'Trouble down in sector nine,' he reported. 'Alden Park. A riot.'

'How bad?'

'Two dead that we know of. The police have moved in to contain the disturbance.'

'Who is involved?'

'Some students. They were giving a free performance of an historical event when, according to reports, they seemed to go crazy.'

'Right,' snapped Weyburn. 'Get me a copter. Have it on the roof in two minutes.' To Kennedy he said, 'Let's see what's going on.'

From above they looked like ants, milling, running, merging to break and reform ever-new patterns. Young people oddly dressed, seeming to be the participants in a fancy dress charade, a fragment of history resurrected in a modern age. Limp bodies lay on the grass close to a sparkling fountain, blood ugly as it stained the grass. Ringing them, a line of police stood at a respectful distance, armed and watchful, unsure of what to do.

'Land,' said Weyburn to the pilot. 'Close to that officer.'

The man was worried, his forehead creased, eyes nervous as he looked beyond his men at the screaming crowd. Others stood far back, civilians, none certain whether this was a part of the performance or something more serious. The fallen could have been play-acting; the blood could have been a harmless stain. Similar student performances were common in the city, entertainment and education enjoyed by adults and children alike.

3   33

Kennedy said, 'What happened?'

He was a civilian, unknown to the officer. He glanced at Weyburn, received a nod, and said, 'We don't rightly know. The students were putting on a depiction of a Sioux ghost dance. You know, drums, chanting, dancing in a circle, that kind of thing. I guess they must have got hysterical because suddenly they started to fight. The local officer called for help, but before it could come a couple had been killed. I arrived about then and called for more men to seal the disturbance.'

Kennedy nodded and glanced beyond the police to where the students were milling. They wore beads, paint and feathers, strips of synthetic hide, and carried crude weapons of wood and stone. Some of them were smeared with blood.

'Send for gas,' snapped Weyburn. 'Have copters come and drench the area. You should have done it right away.'

'Wait!' Kennedy gestured toward the students. 'The urgency is gone. They aren't hurting each other now. Are your men armed with anesthetic guns?'

'Of course. We couldn't use bullets against kids.'

'Have marksmen stand ready. If anyone looks as if they're going to attack anyone, bring them down.'

Weyburn frowned. 'Cap?'

'Something's happened. Maybe a mistake or another test. Students are wild but they don't go kill-crazy. My guess is that something made them that way.' To the officer he said, 'This ceremony they were performing. Do they all drink out of the same bowl?'

'I don't know.'

'Find out. And see if you can spot a container of some kind on the grass. A fumigating bomb, perhaps, something like that.'

'A gas,' said Weyburn, understanding. 'A vapor blasted from a can which had been thrown among them. Some would have got it, others not. But who, Cap? And why?'

Two questions, one of which couldn't be answered yet, but Kennedy had a shrewd suspicion of the reason behind the riot. Once at the party, the second time in the girl's apartment, and now this. Sure bait to bring Weyburn running; and it was highly probable that he would not have come alone.

Kennedy turned, eyes searching the watching crowd. He caught a glimpse of a familiarly shaped head, shoulders which he had seen before. As he moved toward the figure he noted the nondescript features of the man he had seen in the library.

He turned as Kennedy approached and for a moment their eyes met. His eyes belied his features; they were cold, hard, filled with a smoldering resentment. They widened a little as he recognized Kennedy's intention and then, in a sudden explosion of energy, he was running, one hand diving beneath his blouse, reappearing weighted with a pistol.

Kennedy lunged after him. A child ran between them and he jumped over the small figure, dodged around a gaping woman, throwing himself down as the man turned and fired. A thread of flame spouted from the muzzle of the weapon, the self-propelled missile exploding against the bole of a tree. Another took a man in the chest, bursting open his ribs and shredding his lungs in a shower of blood and ruptured tissue.

Before Kennedy could rise the man was running again, directly toward the ring of police, his arm lifted, the gun aimed directly as Weyburn.

The Director fired first. He looked down at the dead man, at the neat hole between his eyes, and said, as Kennedy joined him, 'That was a mistake. Now he can't tell us anything.'

'If he could you'd be dead now.'

'Maybe, but I should have winged him.' Weyburn looked at the gun in his hand and irritably thrust it back into the holster beneath his tunic. 'Another dead end. Well, let's clear up the mess.'

The riot was over. Students sat around, faces blank, eyes dull. A little group of girls sobbed as they clung together for mutual support. Police moved among them, taking the crude weapons, ushering them to where a line of ambulances waited. One of the policemen came to where Kennedy stood with the Director. He held an open can in his hand.

'We found this,' he said. 'Right in the middle of where they were dancing.'

Kennedy looked inside and saw flame-scorched metal. Chemicals had burned the interior clean of anything it may have contained. The rest had been absorbed, dissipated, lost in the air.

'A test,' he said, 'but not an effective one. The drug wasn't strong enough and the effects didn't last. My guess is that you were the real target.'

Weyburn frowned. 'Me?'

'If I had been doped I could have attacked you at the reception. You ignored me for reasons we both know, but to anyone watching it would have been a fair guess that I felt resentment. You could have gone to check out the girl. It was almost certain that you would investigate the riot.' Kennedy paused, then added, slowly, 'And a lot of people know that you are the Director of Terran Control.'

Too many. Back in his office Weyburn paced the floor, scowling. Luden was present; he had arrived while the others were at the riot. Now he sat, his grave features thoughtful as Kennedy brought him up to date.

A most distressing situation,' he commented. 'It seems obvious that any power wishing to weaken Terran Control would strike at the head of the department. I would suggest, Director, that you take all precautions against another such attack.'

'How?' demanded Weyburn. 'Everyone around me has been checked and tested a dozen times. I can stay in this office, true, but I'm damned if I'm going to live like a prisoner from now on.'

'Even so you must be careful,' insisted Luden. 'Eat and drink nothing which does not come from a sealed container. If possible have someone taste everything first. A return to medievalism, perhaps, but certain old institutions have their value.'

'I'll settle for sealed containers. But I need more than that. I've got to find out who is behind all this.'

Kenndy said, 'Did you discover anything, Jarl?'

'Very little of real value, Cap. Dr Wuhun was most obliging, but he has had very little success with his experiments and his staff has remained with him for the past few years. There have been a few visitors, mostly in the field of brain surgery; all local. Madam Chee's accomplishments have been sporadic; apparent success followed by inexplicable failure. However, she did have a visit from a Chambonian. He wanted to investigate psychological behavior patterns and the physical and mental changes caused in the human organism by conditions of extreme stress. He stayed for several weeks and left about a year ago.'

'A Chambodian!' Weyburn paused in his restless pacing. 'His name?'

'Ser Prome. A scientist of limited reputation who was unable to obtain research facilities on his home world.' Luden added,

36

'He had an assistant. A native of Merah. Yuah Taiyan. It seems that he had a certain telepathic ability unusual in humanoids. Madam Chee was sorry to see him go.'

'A telepath.' Kennedy was thoughtful. 'How good was his ability?'

'Very good indeed. He could not emit, only receive, but when in fairly close proximity to his subject, he was remarkably accurate. Madam Chee found him most helpful.' Luden added, shrewdly, 'I think I know what's in your mind, Cap. However, Yuah Taiyan is no longer on Earth.'

'We can find him.'

Weyburn said, 'Wait a minute, Cap. What is all this about?'

'As far as we know Chambodia is working through Merah against the Terran Sphere. Yuah Taiyan is a Merahinian and, as a telepath, he must have picked up information of some kind. Once we find him he could lead us straight to where we want to go.'

'True,' admitted Weyburn. 'If we can find him.'

'He's probably back on Merah. Find out what you can while we're on our way. The *Mordain* is ready. Come on, Jarl, let's get into space.'

CHAPTER SIX

Penza Saratov was restless. He prowled the *Mordain* like a disconsolate ghost, checking, rechecking, his big hands deft as he made minor adjustments to the coils of the engine.

'We should have had more time, Cap,' he grumbled. 'Those technicians back on Earth can't be trusted to do a good job. I almost had a fight with one when he insisted that the coils had been tuned to peak standard.'

Kennedy smiled. 'And had they?'

'Yes,' admitted Penza. 'But he was talking about an ordinary ship. I couldn't get it through to him that the *Mordain* is no ordinary vessel.'

As he was no ordinary man. Almost as wide as he was tall, the shaven ball of his head running into a thick neck mounted on massive shoulders, he looked something like a troglodyte from Earth's ancient mythology. Arms, torso, thighs, and calves completed the picture of a living machine of flesh, bone, and muscle. A giant born, raised, and trained on a world with three times the normal gravity of Earth.

'We should have had another week at least,' he continued. 'I wanted full tests under battle conditions. Listen to that engine!' He cocked his head. 'Still not right!'

Right, to Penza, meant perfect, and he would accept nothing less. Kennedy left him to it, moving forward to where Chemile stood watch at the controls. At first glance the compartment appeared empty, then a portion of the bulkhead seemed to shift and move, stepping forward to reveal the figure of a man.

'Practicing again, Veem?'

'That's right, Cap. I've got to keep in condition. Did I tell you about that time on Earth during a lecture when fifty women tried to find me and failed?'

'Yes,' said Kennedy. 'Often.'

'And when Jarl was talking to Dr Wuhun and I slipped past into his private office and checked his files?'

'You did.'

'Practice,' said Chemile smugly. 'I don't care what Penza says, a man has to keep in condition. The trouble is, Cap, that he gets a little jealous of my skill. I mean, he can bend iron bars and all that, but could he hide in a crowd? You know he couldn't. Now he keeps saying that I should do all the work while he messes about with the engine. He doesn't understand that a man of a sensitive nature can't take an interest in cooking and all that.'

Kennedy sighed. Chemile, obviously, had been spoiled by his sojourn on Earth.

'Someone has to do it, Veem.'

'We should take turns.'

'You're best at it,' soothed Kennedy. 'It takes an artist to produce a good meal. Penza won't admit it, but he knows that he couldn't equal you if he tried. And he is busy. We all want the ship to be in optimum condition.'

Veem Chemile was tall, thin, with a roach of hair over a sloping brow, eyes which were tiny points in the smooth ovoid of his face. His ears were small, tight to his skull, pointed like those of a cat. There was much about him reminiscent of a feline. The way in which he moved, his quietness, his ability to remain motionless for long periods of time, resting in a strange comatose state while his skin, scaled with minute flecks of photosensitive tissue, adopted the coloration of the background against which he stood.

A man-sized chameleon with an infinitely superior protective mechanism developed on the harsh world which had given him birth. Consciously controlled and amazingly adaptable.

Now he said, 'I guess you're right, Cap. Each to the thing he does best. Penza is good with engines and I'm good at other things.'

Navigating for one. Kennedy checked the instruments, then went back to where Luden sat in his compact laboratory. He had his notebook open before him, transferring his notations to a big volume of cross-references. Without looking up he said, 'This is amazing, Cap. I am certain now that the symbols found on that old Incan temple have a correlation with the Zheltyana Sign. And there is a significant mention in a Chinese manuscript which has an echo in one of the Indian Vedas.'

'Bearing on the Zheltyana?' The enigma of the Ancient Race which had left artifacts scattered on a host of worlds had engrossed Kennedy for as long as he could remember. Long before men had climbed from the sea a civilization had touched the Galaxy to flower and vanish, leaving only fragmentary signs of their existence. It was his dream that, one day, he would be able to discover the secret of the Ancient Race.

'Unfortunately the possibility is too remote for serious consideration,' said Luden regretfully. 'The time element is against it. However, the old records could have been influenced by a race which may have had some knowledge of distant events. For example, the Quendial Artifacts have never satisfactorily been explained. Their location presents a paradox. Yet if we assume that they may have been left by a race which came along after the Zheltyana no paradox exists. The relatively thin surface deposits could be of fairly recent origin.'

'Moved from their original location?' Kennedy shook his head. 'I doubt it, Jarl. In that case we have to assume that the race which moved them also vanished. Possible, but unlikely.'

'Even so the probability must not be dismissed. We know that some races had space travel before we did. The Chambodians for one. A trading vessel could have found the Artifacts, moved them and, perhaps, later dumped them to make room for a more profitable cargo. Just as an alien vessel could have reached Earth back in prehistory, found nothing but primitive peoples, and left never to return. The early legends cannot be ignored, Cap. They carry a message, now blurred with time and retelling, but with a grain of truth somewhere in their content.'

A field of fascinating speculation, but there was no time to delve into it now. From a speaker set against the wall came Chemile's voice.

'Cap, we've got company.'

He gestured to the screens as Kennedy joined him in the control room. A tiny fleck showed against the graduated panel. Beyond and around it shone the points of light, the sheets of glowing brilliance, the murky patches of interstellar space.

'Full magnification, Veem?'

'Yes, Cap. I spotted it first on the Larvik-Shaw space disturbance detector. Something is out there and it isn't natural. It has to be a ship.'

'Slow down,' ordered Kennedy. 'If it's following us it will get in closer and we may be able to spot what type it is.'

Chemile nodded and reached for the controls. The *Mordain* slowed a little, and the tiny fleck grew larger, taking on shape and recognizable form. A Chambodian vessel armed and armored, a military scout devoid of markings, but unmistakable to Kennedy's experienced eye. It had no right to be in the Terran Sphere, but space was vast and the possibility of is discovery remote.

'It could be coincidence,' said Chemile dubiously. 'We both just could be happening to be going the same way.'

It was possible, coincidences happened, but Kennedy distrusted them when they did. He stood, watching the screens, calculating time and distance. The alien ship came closer, slowing to match the velocity of the *Mordain*, grim and menacing against the stars.

He said, 'We'll give them a chance, Veem. Drop out of hydrive, change course ninety degrees for three minutes, alter back, and engage hydrive again.'

'Right, Cap.'

The stars flickered as the *Mordain* fell below the velocity of light, seeming to jerk, colors changing, the faint background haze of hyspace vanishing to be replaced by the starkness of the normal universe. Chemile waited, ignoring Penza's voice as he called from the engine room.

'Veem! What the hell are you doing? How can I adjust the coils while you keep changing velocity?'

'Emergency, Penza,' snapped Kennedy. 'Stay clear of the engine.'

'Trouble, Cap?' Saratov's voice boomed over the speakers.

'We're not sure yet. Stand by.'

Chemile touched the controls, restoring their original course, then sent the ship back into hydrive again.

'Lost them,' he said triumphantly. 'That ship's gone, Cap.'

He had spoken too soon. The Larvik-Shaw gave a note of warning, a red lamp flashing as the bell chimed, convoluted lines writhing to a central node on its detector panel. On the main screens the fleck reappeared, moving close as they recognized the familiar shape.

Kennedy said, 'How far to the edge of the Terran Sphere, Veem?'

41

'A few minutes at this velocity, Cap. You think they are going to attack us?'

'They aren't following us for fun. My guess is that they are waiting until we enter Merahinian space. They might want to board and confiscate the *Mordain*. They could cripple us and claim we were smuggling contraband or refused to obey a signal. A mistake, of course, and they might even apologize. They could even take us over to the Chambodian Complex.'

Chemile said, 'We could outrun them, Cap.'

It was a possibility. The *Mordain* was the fastest ship in space, but the alien craft was too close and a lucky shot could reach them before they were out of range. There was a better way.

'Combat pattern, Veem,' ordered Kennedy. 'We'll hit while they're still in the Terran Sphere. Full recording for transmission to Earth.'

He ran to the gun turret as Chemile obeyed, alarm bells ringing as he dropped into the chair. The *Mordain* was armed with self-propelled missiles and a heavy-duty Dione as well as atomic torpedoes. The warheads in the torpedoes would be too destructive; Kennedy had no wish to destroy the vessel and the crew within. It would be enough to slow it and render it harmless.

'Ready, Veem,' he said. 'Direct attack.'

'Here we go, Cap.'

Kennedy watched the firing screen, hands tense on the controls. The small shape of the alien vessel moved abruptly toward the central cross-hairs, swelling as Veem fed power to the engine, sending the *Mordain* like an arrow toward its target. Gouts of flame dotted the hull as Kennedy fired, streams of missiles reaching out to explode against the plating. Against the armor they were almost ineffective, serving only to distract the captain, the gunners, smashing a few scanning eyes, and creating a temporary blindness.

Following them came the blast of the Dione.

Unstable isotopes vented their energy in the firing chamber, the raw energy expelled and focused by the ring of permanent magnets which provided a guiding field. It streaked from the muzzle in a narrow shaft of ravening destruction, hitting the alien ship just behind the nose, sending puffs of volatized metal from the ruptured hull. A Dione handgun could char a hole

42

through the body of a man, incinerate a horse with continued firing. The one aboard the *Mordain* could puddle a house into molten slag with a single shot.

Again he fired, aiming toward the rear, where lay the engines. Two shots, the alien ship very close now, caught unawares by the sudden attack. Plating glowed with white heat, sparkled beneath the impact of missiles, yielded to internal pressures.

And then the *Mordain* was past, streaking away from the ship which could now neither follow nor attack.

From the communicator screen Weyburn said, 'Your report received and filed, Cap. You're positive it was a Chambodian vessel?'

'Either that or one got up to look like it. In any case, it had no markings.'

'Fair enough. If they complain I'll read them the Riot Act, but I doubt if they'll do that. They had no right in the Terran Sphere and they know it. They must have been patrolling to spot anything heading toward Merah. Another sure guide that the world must be the source of our trouble. I've more information on Ser Prome. Madam Chee wasn't the only research psychologist he visited. He spent some time at the Weimar Institute on Syrtis Major.'

'Was Yuah Taiyan with him?'

'Yes, Cap, he was. And if the guy's a telepath we can guess why. Some secrets aren't written down. It's possible that he could have discovered a little knowledge from each of several sources. Put them together and he could have found the answer.'

'We'll know if he did when we find him. Anything more at your end?'

'A little. The man I killed at the riot had a record. He was an entrepreneur of the worst kind. Anything you wanted done he would do – for money. He booby-trapped that girl; we found certain chemicals in his apartment which could have been used to fashion a bomb. The Merahinian trade delegation has gone, and so far there's been no more trouble. I'm having everyone connected with Terran Control checked and counter-checked. It will take time, but if there's a leak we'll find it. The rest is up to you.'

'We'll handle it,' promised Kennedy. 'Once we find Yuah Taiyan we'll know where to hit and whom to take care of.'

'We may,' corrected Luden precisely. 'But the man certainly

does seem to be a key figure and it would be best to interrogate him before taking further action.'

'That may not be easy,' said Weyburn. 'I've had word from our agent on Merah. Yuah Taiyan isn't there. Apparently he did something crazy. He went off-world and killed a couple of men on Evalete without apparent cause. They tried him, found him guilty, and sent him to Zarsh.'

'Zarsh!' Like them all Luden knew of the prison-planet whose main import was that of human life. It was a poor world, willing to accept the responsibility of burdensome prisoners for a fraction of what it would cost richer worlds to maintain and guard their criminal misfits. It was a convenient working arrangement for everyone but the prisoners. Zarsh, a fiercely independent world, was not noted for its gentleness. 'You realize,' he said quietly, 'that no one has ever managed to escape? That the entire government and population are united in their determination to safeguard the planet's reputation and with it their major source of income?'

'I know that,' said Weyburn. 'I'm just telling you where he is.'

CHAPTER SEVEN

Zarsh was a savage world.

Cramped in his seat, Kennedy examined it as the ferry orbited down from the vessel which had brought him to the prison world. He had transhipped from the *Mordain*, adopting the guise of a businessman interested in what he saw. A place of endless desert, scarred with jagged mountains, torn with writhing crevasses. The vegetation was sparse, fields of crops painstakingly irrigated, clumps of scrub clinging to the slopes, stunted trees on the plains, their boles festooned with savage spines. A world of rock and sun and sand. A hard place which bred hard men.

'There!' The man sitting beside Kennedy was short, swarthy, bulging with fat. He pointed with a stubby finger. 'Over there. Did you see it?'

'See what?'

'The prison.' He grunted as the world spun beneath them. 'Never mind. It's gone now. You here on business?'

Kennedy nodded.

'That's what I figured.' The man beamed. He stuck out his hand. It enfolded Kennedy's in a meaty embrace. 'Name's Polgar. I own a ranch close to Zarn. Elgets for meat and hides, and let me tell you those hides are the best natural leather to be found in this part of the Galaxy. You interested in hides?'

'I'm with Intergalactic Trading,' explained Kennedy. 'We're interested in anything which could show a profit.'

It was true enough, and the fact that the company never ran at a loss, managed to pay its representatives fabulous salaries, and seemingly bought rubbish to sell at high profits could have been due to coincidence, business cunning, or both. In fact, it was subsidized by Terran Control and existed for the benefit of resident agents. For every Free Acting Terran Envoy like

Kennedy there were a host of others who lived an apparently normal life, lived well, made contacts – and provided cover, assistance, knowledge, and local aid when necessary.

Polgar looked thoughtful. 'Intergalactic, eh? You've got a factor here, right?'

'Alem Haas. You know him?'

'By sight.' The rancher grinned. 'Maybe I'll get to know him better soon. When you've had a chance to look over those hides of mine I've a feeling you'll be more than interested. Iridescent finish and the texture is as soft as you could wish, a prime article for the luxury trade. When can I expect you?'

Kennedy hesitated, frowning. 'Well, I don't know about that,' he said slowly. 'I'm not here to step on any toes. Haas is a good man, and we like to leave all matters of local business to his judgement. But I'll tell you what I'll do. I'll talk to him about it. Right?'

'You do that.' If Polgar was disappointed he didn't show it. Suddenly he lunged forward, his finger hard against the window. 'There! Now you can see it!'

A long, thin tongue of land thrust itself into the bed of a long-departed sea. On three sides of the plateau the ground fell away in an undercut curve for something like five hundred feet. A thick line of vegetation ran along the edge. In the center of the area sprawled the prison buildings.

Kennedy followed them with his eyes until they fell behind.

'You saw that hedge?' Polgar was eager to please, proud of his knowledge. 'Thorn bushes twenty feet high and a hundred yards thick. They carry spines three inches long and are tipped with nerve poison. Get scratched by one and you'll be in bed for a week. Not even a wild elget could get through it, and they're about as tough as they come.'

Kennedy made no comment, looking through the window. An aerial study of the place was important, one of the reasons he had transshipped.

'You'll see it again soon,' promised the rancher. 'One edge of the landing spiral passes close to the jail. We could even see my ranch; it's pretty close.'

'To the prison area?'

'That's right. Makes it convenient for labor. I've a score of contract men in the field and a couple of women for the house. Fine girls, the pair of them. Good cooks and they know how to mind their place.' His elbow nudged Kennedy in the ribs. 'You want to come out soon and sample the chow? We could even have a party.'

Kennedy smiled with his mouth, his eyes thoughtful, paying no attention to the rancher. He was intent as the ferry went into its landing spiral. The prison wasn't a solid fortress, but a collection of buildings clearly designed to provide maximum protection against the heat. On the land side of the spit a curving barrier of thorns met those along the edge unbroken by any visible gate. Past the barrier on the landward side lay a waste of scarred and broken ground without roads or clearly defined trails. The only real access to the prison was by air.

And he would have bet his life that the innocent-seeming mounds scattered among the buildings and along the line of thorns contained enough anti-air defenses to wreck a fleet.

The ferry landed, Polgar waving farewell as he rolled away to where a cab waited. Kennedy took another, sitting back as the vehicle carried him to the city. Zarn, like the rest of the planet, was a harsh place. The buildings were mostly constructed of fused rock, the roofs wide to shadow the streets, the rooms within high to give added comfort. As the representative of a wealthy company he could afford the best, and took it. A man took his bag to a spacious suite in the Astral Hotel and stood quietly waiting for dismissal. He was slight, dressed in a gray uniform of pants and shirt, a broad collar of silvery metal fastened tightly around his neck. His eyes held the expression of a man for whom there could be no hope.

The collar was responsible for that. Broken, it would inject a two-day poison while at the same time emitting a radio-howl. The same thing could be accomplished by a switch thrown in the prison. If a prisoner tried to escape that switch would be thrown. The poison induced immediate paralysis and cramping agony. None but the desperate had ever tried to escape, and they never did it more than once.

Throwing him a coin, Kennedy said, 'How long have you been here?'

'With respect, sir, such matters are not discussed on Zarsh.'

'I'll put it another way. How long does a prisoner have to wait before being granted the privilege of working outside the compound?'

'That rests with the warden, sir. Never before two years.' The

47

man was restless, unwilling to talk about his situation and, perhaps, risk his position. Yet, as Kennedy knew, most visitors would be curious. As yet he had done nothing outside of his assumed character. 'Is it your wish that I draw your bath?'

'Yes,' said Kennedy. 'Make it cold. Is it always as hot as this?'

'Hotter, sir. Summer has still to reach its zenith.'

'You'd better bring me some wine,' said Kennedy. A businessman relaxing after a long trip would be eager for comfort. 'And a menu. Is there anything special you can recommend?'

'The elget steak is very good, sir. And the ourtag fruit is in season. Will you eat here, sir, or in the dining room downstairs?'

'Downstairs, later. Is the hotel very full?'

'Quite full, sir. We have many sportsmen who have arrived for the hunt.'

'The hunt?'

'Yes, sir.' The man's mouth looked as if it had tasted something vile. 'A prisoner, Yuah Taiyan, has volunteered for quarry.'

He was small with a round head which seemed too large for his shoulders and the slight body beneath. His lips were full above a vestige of a chin and his eyes looked like those of a beaten dog. He was boyish, insignificant, painfully fragile. He did not look like a murderer.

Warden Lumac was not deluded. He had long since discarded any notion he may have held as to the physical characteristics of criminals together with any sympathy he may have had toward their crimes. Fifty years on Zarsh, thirty of them in the prison service, ten as warden, had turned him into a machine. And the record was plain. Yuah Taiyan had murdered two men and had been sentenced under due process of Evaletian law to spend the remainder of his natural life in confinement.

And yet even a convicted murderer should be prevented from committing ugly suicide.

'You have made an official application to become recognized quarry,' said Lumac. His voice, like his face, was emotionless. 'I am giving you a final opportunity to reconsider the matter. The regulations provide for this because we understand the ignorance under which you may have made the application. Do you understand?'

'Yes, sir.'

Taiyan spoke in little more than a whisper. It seemed incredible that he should ever shout or deal in naked violence, but twenty-seven people had watched him commit double-murder. He had killed two men ascending in a public transport, smashing their skulls with a bottle he had snatched from a woman's shopping bag, acting too fast to be stopped. He'd had no chance of escaping and he had made no attempt to do the impossible. To Lumac it was amazing that anyone could be so stupid, but then, if criminals weren't stupid, they would never be caught.

He gestured toward a chair. 'You may sit.' He added, as the prisoner obeyed, 'Have you any idea at all of what you are doing?'

The beaten-dog's eyes moved so as to focus on the warden's face. 'Yes, sir.'

'Well?'

'It is the only opportunity I have of ever leaving this planet alive.'

It was true enough, taken in the broadest sense. Only an order of the court which had sentenced him could remit his sentence; obviously he did not expect any such order. Curiously the warden looked at the man where he sat, nondescript in his drab uniform. Taiyan had adapted well since his arrival, the usual small troubles attendant on any new intake, but for him to volunteer as quarry was the last thing Lumac had expected. For a moment he brooded on what the reason could be and then recognized the impossibility of his ever finding out. No one but a prisoner could understand the pressures which drove them.

'I must point out the obvious,' he said patiently. 'In a couple of years or so you may be allowed to work outside. There will be small privileges, some comforts which you lack at the moment, and a certain measure of freedom. Life, while hard, could be more bearable than it is for you at the present. You have considered this?'

'Yes, sir. I have.'

'And you still insist?'

'Yes, sir. I do.'

'Then I must inform you that of the last twenty men to volunteer only one managed to reach sanctuary,' said Lumac evenly. 'He was a native of Somarch. It is a hot, bleak world as

49

close to Zarsh as can be found in this sector of the Galaxy. You come from where?'

'Merah, sir.'

'A soft world.' Rising, the warden stepped to the window and adjusted the polarizing control. The glass brightened to reveal the scene outside, arid ground baking beneath the furnace heat of a swollen sun. Once Zarsh had held seas, wide oceans, and fertile plains, but that had been long ago, the native race which had lived here destroyed beneath the savage heat of an unstable primary. Lumac darkened the pane. 'Out there I doubt if you would last a single day. And you will have more to contend with than the natural hostility. Are you so eager to die?'

Taiyan ran the tip of his tongue over the fullness of his lower lip. 'No, sir.'

'Then why be so foolish? I have accepted your application, but this is your final chance. Continue to insist and there can be no reversal of your decision. Now why not be sensible and forget the whole thing?'

'I can't do that, sir.' The soft voice held a note of desperation. 'I've got to get out. I've got to! I – ' He broke off, swallowing. 'Please, sir. I have the right to volunteer.'

'That is correct.' Lumac reseated himself. How did the man know of his right? A guard, perhaps, or another prisoner could have told him. He knew, that was all that mattered; the warden was a hard but honest man. And old traditions had to be preserved. 'It is a residue from the old days,' he explained. 'A man needs a fantastically high survival factor in order to escape from this place. The early settlers knew better than to eliminate such a trait. For the sake of his genes a successful volunteer was forgiven his crimes. He became a citizen of Zarsh and received compensation. Some of them reached high position. All were given the opportunity to father many children.'

His voice held the pride of ancestry.

'But that was in the old days when the men held here were hardier than they are now. Believe me when I tell you that, as things stand, you have literally no chance at all. Once you pass the barrier you will be going to certain death.'

He meant it. He believed it, but Yuah Taiyan dared not. No reasoning creature could sanely accept the inevitability of its own destruction. He said, 'With respect, sir, a five percent chance of success is not a certainty of failure.'

Lumac was patient. 'When I said that of the last twenty volunteers only one had managed to reach sanctuary I should have added that even he died of wounds and exposure within thirty hours. Nineteen failures from nineteen attempts is a record of one hundred percent failure. Twenty deaths from the same number of volunteers is the same. Do you wish to reconsider?'

'No, sir. My mind is made up.'

'As you wish.' Lumac had done his best and there were those outside who would not thank him for having tried at all. The hunters who thirsted for sport and potential gain. The sportsmen, so called, who were eager to kill a defenseless prey. The ones who made wagers, not on the quarry's chances – they knew better – but on how long he would last and who would win. The merchants and shopkeepers who would gain from the sale of equipment and souvenirs. The vintners, the hoteliers, the ones who sold food and entertainment.

Well, he had tried, and his failure would help to fill the coffers of Zarsh. Lumac thumbed a button and to the guard who answered the summons said, 'Take the prisoner back to his duties.'

His eyes were bleak as he watched the dead man walk away.

CHAPTER EIGHT

Chon Selman hefted the rifle, running his hands over the stock, the universal sight. He worked the action and studied the ammunition. Each missile packed enough energy to blast a hole through a twenty-inch brick wall at a thousand yards. The gun was warranted to be accurate to within an inch at the same distance. It cost more than he had earned in the past year.

'A nice weapon,' he commented.

'The best.' Aihun Zemao was sweating. All new arrivals to Zarsh sweated for a time. 'It could be yours.'

Selman slowly fed the ammunition back into the magazine.

'You're a hunter,' said the Merahinian. 'I'm told that you're one of the best.'

'Whoever told you that didn't lie.'

Aihun Zemao said nothing, looking around the room in which they sat. It was of the universal fused rock, the floor bare, the only decoration an elget skin stretched against one wall. A cot, unmade, stood in a corner. A cabinet, open, showed a scanty wardrobe. The wine he had been offered as a guest had been thin, watered, acid to the tongue. The hunter himself matched the picture. Selman was gaunt, his cheekbones prominent. He wore a tunic of faded elget skin. His pants, like his boots, showed signs of wear.

He said, harshly, 'I've had bad luck. A broken leg on a trip to the Shuman Hills. They had to carry me back. It cost me.'

'Of course,' soothed Zemao. 'I understand. Tell me: have you ever hunted men?'

'Quarry?' Selman closed the action, snapped on the safety, and set the rifle to one side. 'A few times, yes.'

'And gained the trophy?'

'Twice.'

Zemao raised his eyebrows.

'That's double what anyone else has managed.'

'But surely, a man with such a high reputation – ?' Zemao broke off on the question, leaving the doubt unspoken.

'You don't know much about the hunt,' said Selman. 'That's obvious. First off, I wasn't alone. Those who stalk quarry never are. It isn't like going after a wild elget or a klarg. A quarry hunt is about the most vicious thing you can imagine. Not the prey, that's nothing, but the other hunters. Everyone is against you and you can never be certain that you aren't in someone's sights. You can't even be sure the quarry is in your sector. You've got to scout around and, if you get too far ahead, you'll collect a bullet in the back. I've seen it happen.'

'And done it yourself?'

'Maybe.' Selman was curt. 'In the open ground anything goes. Just what do you want, mister?'

Aihum Zemao scowled. He didn't like what he was doing nor the orders that he had been given. They had reached him shortly after he had left Earth with the trade mission and he considered the errand beneath his dignity. Lumac hadn't helped. The warden had been polite but firm. Zarsh had accepted the Taiyan contract, but Zarsh had its own laws and custom had to be maintained. The prisoner had claimed his right to be quarry and that right would be protected. Courtesy had caused the warden to notify Evalete as to the development and they, in turn, had passed the information to Merah as the prisoner's home world. As the representative of that world Aihun Zemao was welcome, but there could be no question of releasing the prisoner into his custody, nor of refusing his request. However, the warden had assured his visitor that there was no question that the quarry could escape. It was inconceivable that he should reach sanctuary.

Aihun Zemao intended to make sure of that.

'A prisoner has volunteered for quarry,' he said abruptly. 'His name is Yuah Taiyan.' He watched for a reaction. None came; the name obviously meant nothing to the hunter. 'I want to hire you for the hunt. It is important that the man does not escape.'

'He won't.'

'Even so I must be certain. Can you arrange it?'

Selman pursed his lips. 'With money, yes.'

'You shall have money. When the man is dead you shall have more. Double the official prize.'

'And the trophy?'

'That shall be mine.' Zemao was grim; there were those who wouldn't be satisfied until they had actual proof. 'But I must insist that there be no possibility of failure. That rifle will help you to succeed.'

Selman picked up the weapon, his hands caressing it as if it were a woman. Reluctantly he shook his head. 'No.'

'Why not? It is a good weapon.'

'Too good. It would never be allowed. The quarry is given his chance,' explained the hunter. 'Not much of one, but a chance all the same. No explosive missiles, no lasguns, no Diones, nothing but a short-range weapon with open sights. To use anything else would be outright murder.'

'A fine distinction,' said Zemao dryly. 'Well, no matter as long as the man dies. It would be best, I think, if I were to join you. In any case it would be an interesting experience.'

'Interesting.' Selam looked down at his hands. Things were hard and he needed the work. 'Tell me: have you any imagination?'

'Why?'

'I was just wondering. Have you ever stopped to think how that poor devil in the prison must be feeling?'

'No, and I suggest that you do not concern yourself with such matters.' The Merahinian stepped toward the door. 'Regard him as you regarded that beast whose skin hangs on your wall. Something to be slain for profit. I'm sure that it will steady your aim.'

He couldn't understand. None of the soft fools who came to kill beasts under his guidance could understand. There was no joy in hunting creatures you couldn't respect. Selman crossed to where the skin hung on the wall, touching it, letting his hand run over the shimmering surface. It would make new pants, a new shirt, but he never thought of using it for that. It had come from a beast which had almost killed him, the leader of a group he had hunted in the mountains for a solid week. His first shot had missed; the second only made a superficial wound. He had fired again as the tail had smashed at his ribs, falling as the elget had fallen, living as the creature died. He had crawled two miles coughing blood, later to return and claim the hide.

A man could respect a beast like that, something which had the ability to strike back, to defend itself. What kind of quarry would a helpless man be? But an unarmed prisoner would be desperate and perhaps the most dangerous creature of all.

And the others, those who would contest his right to the trophy: They could kill more surely than a beast and they shared his own intelligence and cunning.

Selman wondered how the prisoner felt.

Yuah Taiyan could have told him. The waiting was the hard part. During the day when he was kept busy there was little time for thought, but at night, when settling to sleep, there was no escape. Always the noise came to smash past his defenses. The dull, endless, hopeless noise from the minds of those around him.

Moaning, he rolled on his bunk.

'Getting the jitters?' a man whispered from the shadows. His voice held concern but his mind was engrossed with red hunger. How long would he last? How soon would he die? What would be the manner of his going? 'It won't be long now. When you pass the barrier keep a sharp watch for fren. They're worse than the hunters, but you won't have to worry about them until you get near sanctuary. Fren are all over. Lean against a rock and one could sting you. If one does your only hope is to bite out the place where the poison entered. A good, deep bite. Of course, if you get stung in the back, that could be difficult.'

'Shut up, Maelk,' a second voice said, deep, harsh, but the mind held sadness. 'The guy's got enough on his plate without you worrying him.'

'I was only trying to help.'

'Like hell, you were.' A third voice, high-pitched with strain, the mind a turmoil of conflicting echoes. 'That help he can do without. If you're so smart why don't you volunteer?'

'Being smart isn't being stupid. I know my own limitations, but Taiyan here is different. He wants to go and I figure he needs all the help he can get. Don't forget I've been here a long time. I've seen quarry go out before and I've seen them when they come back.' His mind radiated obscene images colored by his imagination, but based on truth. Limp shapes returned for disposal. Those who had tried and failed. Dead. Incomplete. Did they always remove the heads?

The man with the harsh voice said, 'Pay him no attention, Yuah. You'll make it. Lumac's doing his best to give you a chance. That's why he's working you so hard. Getting you as tough as possible in the time left. It's his way of helping out.'

The words were meant to comfort, but the thought which accompanied them revealed the truth:

You poor devil. You haven't got a chance!

'Of giving the hunters a run for their money, you mean.' Maelk's voice held a sneer, his mind a sick envy. *Why couldn't I be out there with them? Waiting, watching to catch the quarry. To bring it down, take the trophy, and collect the prize.* His voice above his stream of thought. 'What good is a quarry that simply lays down and dies? You know what I think? The best thing Yuah could do is to find a good sharp rock and open a vein. Just sit down somewhere and take it easy until he dies. That'd rob the hunters of their fun.'

'Shut up, Maelk. I'm not going to tell you again.'

Farther down the dormitory a man turned and muttered in his sleep. Yuah Taiyan cringed at the impact of murderous anger, the residue of nightmare, an incoherent burst of primeval fury. And it was loud. Loud!

He moaned again, hands clamped uselessly to his ears. Always it had been like this, but always before there had been a medium of escape. Distance, solitude, personal discipline, all had helped to muffle and dissipate the ceaseless noise. The thoughts radiated from a host of minds which he could catch and, to a degree, filter, gaining coherent sense from the welter of mental sound. But here there could be none of that. In prison he was in too close a proximity with too many others. He could do nothing but remain constantly aware of the flood of thoughts, and that very proximity accentuated their impact.

Unless he could escape he would go insane.

'Yuah.' The man with the harsh voice was beside him, a clot of shadow in the dimness. 'Listen. I've been on hot worlds before. Remember to take things easy. You've all the time in the world. Suck a pebble to ease your thirst and don't move too fast or you'll sweat too much. Don't worry too much about the fren. They're there, but you can dodge them. Try to find somewhere sheltered and rest during the day. Move at night and, when you get in sight of sanctuary, try to find a hunter. If you do, sneak up on him and smash in his head.'

'Kill the bloodthirsty swine before he kills you!'

The savagery of the thought roared in his mind like the blast of a siren. Yuah flinched.

'Something wrong?'

'No. No, it's just that – '

'You're tense,' said the man. 'Maybe too tense, and that can be bad. Try to relax once you're on your way. And remember that we all want you to make it. Maybe, if you do, others will try.' His hand dropped, squeezed a shoulder. His thoughts radiated pity. 'Get some sleep now. You're going to need all the strength you can find.'

A friend, thought Yuah, a sympathizer, but he was on the wrong side of the wall. He lay, dreaming of ships and men who would come from the skies to overpower the guards and snatch him to freedom. A wish which would never be realized. He was alone. In a sense he had always been alone. The thoughts he had received from others had never held more than a detached curiosity as far as he was concerned. Even the Chambodian had let him down.

Restlessly he turned, trying to ignore the beating roar of mental sound, the inescapable choice he had made. Death of the body or death of the mind? At least, if he should die, he would finally know peace.

CHAPTER NINE

The elgat steak was as promised and the ourtag fruit held a delicious succulence which blended well with the wine, but the news was bad.

'Quarry.' Kennedy leaned back in his chair and stared at his guest. 'What made him do it?'

Alem Haas shrugged. He was neatly dressed in thin fabrics of dull maroon, the color blending well with the olive of his skin. 'Who knows? He could be desperate and willing to take the chance. In any case, Cap, there's nothing we can do. The game has to be played according to the rules.'

Rules, perhaps, which could be manipulated. Kennedy frowned, thinking. The *Mordain* was in orbit, but he already knew that an outright attack was out of the question. Even if he summoned the others there was little they could do. The time was too short. Neither Penza Saratov nor Veem Chemile could use their special talents and Luden's sharp mind could add little to what he had already determined. Somehow Yuah Taiyan had to be saved from the trap which he had voluntarily entered.

Alem Haas shrugged when he mentioned it. 'I don't see how it can be done, Cap. The hunt has attracted a lot of people and the prize will be high. We could bribe some but not all, and it will take only one bullet to bring him down.'

He turned as music cut the air. A troupe of jugglers moved onto the floor, knives flashing as they tested their skill against needle points and razor edges. A small mixed party entered the restaurant where they sat, the artificially cooled dining room of the Astral Hotel. A waiter guided them to a table. Another came toward where Kennedy sat with the local agent. He was courteous, but his intention was plain. He wanted their table.

'Have you finished your meal, gentlemen? If so, perhaps you would care to watch the entertainment from the balcony. The air is cooler there and the view superb.'

Haas said, 'You are busy tonight.'

'Very busy, sir. In normal times, as you know, you would not be troubled, but as there is such a demand the management hopes that you will understand. A bottle of wine will be provided, with our compliments, for your pleasure.'

Kennedy rose. As a resident Alem Haas could have insisted on remaining at the table, but he could not afford to be other than cooperative. At the foot of the stairs leading to the balcony Kennedy halted, turning to look back at their table. Aihun Zemao was just about to sit down.

'Cap?' The agent was waiting. 'Let's enjoy the free wine.'

'Forget it. Let's go to your office.'

On the way Kennedy sat back, brooding. The Merahinian could not be on Zarsh by accident. The only thing which would have attracted him was the hunt, which meant that for Merah the quarry held a special interest. Had he arranged for the man to volunteer? A bribed guard could have radiated the message, but Kennedy didn't think it likely. While in jail the man was safely out of the way.

As the factor led the way into his inner office, Kennedy said, 'Exactly how long do we have before the hunt begins?'

'Not more than a few hours. Local notice is at the discretion of the warden and the only stipulation is that the attempt must be made within twenty days of the initial application. That expires the day after tomorrow. From what I gather Lumac has stretched it to the limit.'

'Why?'

Haas shrugged. 'Who knows? Maybe he wants to give the man the best chance he can. Or maybe he wanted to spread the word so as to attract a good crowd.'

The agent had been contaminated by the hardness of his adopted world. Hunters would bring money and, to Zarsh, money was always important. The reason didn't matter, but the delay had given time to the Merahinian to make any arrangements he chose.

'Aihun Zemao is here,' said Kennedy. 'My guess is that he wants to make sure the quarry doesn't make it. Is there any way we can spike his guns?'

'No.' Haas was emphatic. 'The hunt is wide open,' he explained. 'I can bid high for a few sectors, but that won't stop

59

him if he has money to spend. Frankly, I don't think Yuah Taiyan stands a chance.'

'Then we'll have to give him one.' Kennedy crossed to where a detailed map hung against a wall. He studied it, eyes narrowed, hand lifting to touch various spots, the prison area, the city, a line of vivid blue. 'What's this?'

'The sanctuary area.'

'And this?' Kennedy touched a spot close to the blue line.

'Polgar's ranch. He breeds elgets for hides and meat.'

'Polgar,' said Kennedy thoughtfully. 'I've met him. I think we should pay him a visit.'

'Now?' It was past midnight.

'First thing tomorrow. Let him know we're coming. Tell him that you're interested in his hides.' Kennedy resumed his study of the map. 'And get me all the information you have on the hunt, the local hunters, and the habits of elgets.'

The ranch was a boulder-strewn area of sand and thorn. The ranch house was of the usual fused rock, the roof planted with irrigated sward for coolness. A warehouse and power plant stood to one side together with a row of shacks which looked more like ovens than homes. A sonic barrier enclosed the ranch boundaries, the line marked by flaring red dye bonded to the soil. Polgar was waiting when they arrived. He came forward, grinning, his hand extended as they jumped from the cab.

'I knew it,' he chortled. 'A good businessman can smell a profit a mile away. Just wait till you see those hides!'

He turned, shouting orders. Two men wearing silver collars jumped to obey, opening the doors of the warehouse, standing deferentially by as the fat rancher displayed his wares. The skins were nothing special, but Kennedy had his own reasons for wanting to do business.

'Nice,' he commented. 'I've seen better, but we might be able to use them. What do you think, Alem?'

The agent looked dubious. He fingered a hide and reached for another. 'Well –'

'You're thinking of the supply angle.' Kennedy nodded. 'A good point. It's no good creating a demand unless we are sure of a supply.' To Polgar he said, 'What is your potential?'

'I've three hundred head, about half ready for slaughter. And there are two hundred hides ready for shipment. If we make a deal I can treble the output within three months.' The rancher caught the glance Kennedy gave Haas. 'Something wrong?'

'Maybe,' said Kennedy. 'What's wrong with the hides that you've had to store them for so long?'

'I was let down. And you have to slaughter the elgets before the skins get too tough. There's nothing wrong with the merchandise.'

'I'll take your word for it. But I've got to be sure of the rest. When can I see them?'

Polgar blinked. 'You want to see the beasts?'

'That's right. How else am I going to be sure you can deliver?' Kennedy glanced at Haas and lowered his voice. 'Look,' he whispered. 'I've overridden the factor on this. He wasn't too keen, said you were unreliable as regards delivery. If you've got the elgets I want to see them. If not, just forget the whole deal.'

'I've got them.'

'Then I'll tell you what. Have them assembled by the south fence tomorrow. Keep them there until I arrive. If I like what I see we'll do business. Right?'

'Tomorrow?' Polgar hesitated. 'That's the day of the hunt.'

'What of it?'

'Nothing,' said Polgar hastily. Cash in hand was better than vicarious pleasure – which was all he'd get if he watched the start. 'Nothing at all. Now that you're here, would you like to look around?'

Kennedy would have demanded that had the offer not been made. He led the rancher to one side, away from Alem Haas, who showed deep interest in the power plant, the mechanism of the sonic barrier and the silver-collared workers who looked after the fat man with smoldering hatred.

On the way back to the city the factor said, 'It can be done, Cap. The only thing is that someone will have to get in there. The contract men can't be bribed; they're too scared of losing their privileges. They hate Polgar but I daren't ask them to act.'

'Never mind,' said Kennedy. Chemile would do what had to be done. 'Just make sure you get me a place on the line with the other hunters.' He smiled, relaxing. 'Tomorrow is going to be a busy day.'

It dawned bright and clear as always, the sun already baking the ground as it rose above the horizon. An hour later the hunters assembled at the starting point. Sanctuary was a thousand yards of cleared sand with observation towers at each end. At night floodlights illuminated the area. Blue dye made a sharp definition.

The hunters were in a festive mood. Bidding for the available places had been high and even though the government took half the proceeds the remainder was well worth winning. Worth getting, too, if the quarry managed to reach sanctuary alive, but no one was taking bets on that remote possibility.

Kennedy spotted Aihun Zemao talking to a gaunt-faced man who wore worn clothing; he recognized Chon Selman from Haas's description. A guard walked past, irritably waving at the crowd.

'Get back there! No contact with the hunters. Get back, I say!'

An umpire followed him, addressing the line of men.

'You all know the rules. If the quarry reaches the blue area he is safe. Should he be shot and fall into it the man responsible will take his place in jail. You have been searched. Weapons and supplies will be given you. Take your places now.'

An attendant moved along the line. He thrust a parcel into Kennedy's hands, receiving in exchange the official token.

'Number seven. Walk down the line and wait.'

Flags marked the various positions. Kennedy lengthened his stride and caught up with the man in the lead.

'Change places?'

'Uh?' The man was suspicious. 'Why?'

'I'm superstitious. Seven is my unlucky number.' It was toward the center, the favored position. 'Swap?'

'Sure.'

No quarry had ever been caught by a man at the edge of the ground and the man probably thought Kennedy a fool. He wasn't. It was good policy to have all his enemies on one side.

A voice boomed from a speaker. 'Pay attention! At the signal you will pass from sanctuary into the open ground. If you see the quarry you may kill it. The one returning with the trophy wins the prize.'

Which, thought Kennedy grimly, was a nice way of putting it. The one who did the actual killing would be certain of nothing but that every other hunter would be after him for the trophy. In the open ground everything went.

The signal was the blast of a gun. As the echoes died the line of men moved forward to the expanse of rugged terrain which sloped upward and quickly carried them from sight. It was an extension of the spit at the far end of which lay the prison; it would narrow the closer they moved toward where the quarry now would be. It was less than a mile across but so torn and heaped with boulders that it provided cover for an army.

Kennedy moved to his extreme left, found a safe niche, and examined the parcel. It contained a slab of concentrate, a small canteen of water, a heavy knife with an eight-inch blade, and a short carbine with three rounds of solid ammunition. The weapon was crudely primitive, inaccurate at any distance, but effective enough at close range. He checked it, loaded it, and put it to one side. From an inner pocket he produced a map of Zarn. He wetted it, and the map faded to sharpen into a large-scale depiction of the open ground.

From Haas he had learned that the hunters usually stationed themselves on the slopes close to the sanctuary. That way they gained the double advantage of a tired and perhaps careless quarry together with less distance to cover with the trophy. But he doubted if Aihun Zemao would stick to accepted practice. He had hired one local and possibly more. They would cover him if he chose to advance, offer a tight defense if he decided to hold his position. They could even now be working to eliminate the opposition.

Kennedy put away his map. He had little choice. It was out of the question for him to stalk and kill all the opposition; the odds were too high against success. All he could do was to travel fast, find Yuah Taiyan, and then guide him back to safety.

He glanced at the sun. Haas would be with Polgar now, killing time, the rancher probably getting more and more impatient. Impatient and a little fearful. Elgets, in mass, were unpredictable and, even when bred, inclined to savage outbursts of rage. They would be milling at the edge of the southern fence, restrained only by the sonic barrier.

Now, thought Kennedy. *Now!*

Chemile had done his work well. Back at the ranch a small package glowed with sudden heat, turning white-hot and fusing the mechanism to which it was attached. The generator took on a new note as it was relieved of its load. Other packages, carefully buried at precise intervals, suddenly vented their energy in nerve-irritating blasts of radiation. Driven by the

CHAPTER TEN

It was, thought Yuah Taiyan, like walking through hell. The old hell of burning fires and endless torments, of eternal thirst and constant anguish. It had commenced the moment he had left the tunnel which penetrated the thorn barrier, the heat rising from naked stone to blast at his eyes and suck moisture from his body. He had tried to follow the advice he had been given, walking slowly, careful were he trod, even finding a stone to suck as he headed toward the north. But the day had passed and a night and now it was another day. He ached with fatigue, the stone long since discarded, one ankle puffed from the sting of some venomous insect. Twice he had almost fallen into the lair of a fren, only his talent enabling him to escape with its warning of danger. And now, he thought, he was going mad.

Tiredly he shook his head, trying to rid it of the ceaseless noise of running water, of cool lakes, fountains, icy glaciers, gentle rain. The pulse of the sea merged with the pound of his heart, the rush of blood in his ears becoming the gush of water from a faucet. The concept of thirst-quenching seemed to fill the universe.

He tripped and fell, the shock of impact just another blow, the ache of bruised flesh just another pain to add to the rest. His lips were cracked, his tongue swollen, his skin febrile, burning to the touch. Squinting, he looked at the sky. The sun was where? North? South? East? West? South, he decided. It had to be south. If not he had been wandering in circles, lost in a maze of narrow canyons, of trails which ran nowhere, of crevasses which closed to reopen in writhing abandon.

Painfully he climbed to his feet. They were bare as was his body aside from the cloth around his loins, blistered from the burning stone despite the training of the past. A wise man would have used the cloth to bind his feet, but he was no longer capable of logical thought. To run, to keep moving, to find the one place where he would be safe: that was all he could think about.

A boulder rose before him and he climbed it, freezing as he reached the summit, mind numbed with a cold ferocity. It was loud, dangerously so; something lurked in the shadows beyond. He turned and moved slowly over the scorching surface, whimpering at the pain from his feet. If he waited night would come and it would be cool. Stars would shine, but starlight gave rise to monstrous shadows which could hide lurking danger. And with the noise in his mind it was hard to concentrate.

The noise!

Tinkling ice and frosted glasses of sweet, white wine. Fruit juice tart and refreshing to the tongue. A waterfall. Showers which stung, like needles, the cool, cool depths of a limpid river. Ponds crusted with lilies and tankards covered with foam. Pearls of rain trickling down a window. And loud. So very loud and therefore so very close.

He fell again and rose, obeying the raw dictates of survival, hobbling over the rocks as he moved toward the source of the mental imagery. Water. He burned for the need of it. He would die without it. In this searing hell it was the only hope he had.

Kennedy watched him come. He leaned against a boulder, his face strained, eyes red with fatigue. For hours he had concentrated on nothing but the concept of water in all its forms. The only sure way to guide the telepath to where he stood.

'Here.' He lifted the canteen. 'You look as if you could use this.'

'No.' Yuah Taiyan backed, his eyes wide with terror. 'No. You're a hunter. You want to kill me.'

'I want to help you. Now have a drink.' The man was like a child; he crumpled as Kennedy reached for his shoulder. Gently he fed a trickle of water into the parched mouth. 'Listen,' he commanded. 'I've come to help you.'

'To kill me.' Yuah Taiyan looked at the knife in Kennedy's belt. 'You want my head for your trophy.'

'Forget that. You're a telepath, right? Well, then, read my mind.'

Taiyan winced. 'Too loud,' he complained. 'You think too loud.' And then, questioningly: 'Earth? You come from Earth?'

'That's right.' Kennedy gave him more water. The canteen

66

had been almost full. 'What happened to you? Why were you arrested?'

'I killed two men. They intended to murder me. I heard them thinking about it. They had a coagulator and had been ordered to eliminate me. I had to kill them in self-defense.'

'Who ordered them to do it? The Chambodian? Ser Prome?'

'You know about him?'

'I know,' said Kennedy grimly. 'He has a secret, hasn't he? You know it and he wanted to shut your mouth. Tell me what it is.'

Taiyan said, helplessly, 'I don't know. His mind was always closed to me. That's what I liked most about working with him. No noise,' he explained. 'With others there is always noise, but never with Ser Prome. And all he wanted was for me to gather scraps of information. It wasn't hard to do. He would get them talking and I would find out the things they thought about but never said. I don't know why he wanted them.'

An idiot, thought Kennedy. A clever child not realizing the use to which his talent could be put. A man whom the Chambodian had used and then discarded. But the reasoning was too facile. There had to be something more.

He said, 'You ran from Merah. Why?'

'I was afraid. Dreadful things happened and I was involved. And I heard them thinking. Ipoh Luang and Marshal Kota Bassein. They wanted no one else to know their secret. Have you more water?'

Kennedy handed him the canteen and slab of concentrate. As yet he had gained little more than he already suspected. Somehow the Chambodian had learned how to negate the censor and had persuaded the military cabal of Merah to use it for their own ends. Yet all Chambodians were distrustful. It was logical to assume that he would have retained the secret, supplying only the finished product. In which case he must have a base from which to operate.

If Yuah Taiyan knew where it was it would account for Aihun Zemao's concern that he should die.

'Tell me,' Kennedy said as the other man lowered the canteen. 'When you were on Merah did you stay with Ser Prome? You did? Where? Describe the place to me.' He listened. 'Right. Was there anywhere else? An isolated building, perhaps?'

It took almost an hour to get the information, probing, select-

67

ing relevant items from a mass of unessential detail, cross-checking and pinpointing locations. Yuah Taiyan had been kept in the dark, but he had learned some things from the minds of the humans with whom he had come into contact. The marshal, his aide, others of the cabal. They had been too cautious. The telepath hadn't realized the importance of what he had learned. He could have been safely left alone.

He said, as Kennedy finished the questioning, 'You've learned all you wanted, haven't you? I can read it in your mind. Are you going to kill me now?'

'Not you,' said Kennedy grimly. 'We're going to get out of here.' He slipped off his shirt and sent the edge of the knife slicing through the material. 'But first let's do something about those feet.'

Progress was easier now that Taiyan's feet were protected. The food had helped, the water still more, but the greatest comfort was knowing that he was not alone. Yuah Taiyan, for the first time, began to feel hope. Then he froze as they entered a gully.

'Is there danger ahead?' Kennedy was at his side, the carbine leveled. 'Where?'

It was a thing like a scorpion which darted from under a rock, sting raised to strike. Kennedy stamped down, chitin crunching beneath the heel of his boot.

'All right. Let's keep moving.'

It would be suicide to hurry and the telepath's skill had its limitations. At short range he could read a person's every thought. At a distance he became confused and could only gain overall impressions. A fren, a lurking insect, a man waiting with a rifle and intent on killing all became the same. Apparently size had nothing to do with the intensity of emotion. But it was the only advantage Kennedy had over the hunters and he had to use it.

He paused as Taiyan gripped his arm.

'Over there.' Taiyan read Kennedy's question. 'A man. Very close. Waiting.'

He lay against the slope of a boulder, his clothing indistinguishable against the stone. A man more ambitious than the rest or perhaps a little more eager to kill. He didn't move as Kennedy crept up behind him, turning too late, lifting his carbine as the butt of Kennedy's rifle slammed down at his skull.

Taiyan said, 'Is he dead?'

'No, but he'll wake with a headache.' Kennedy unloaded the carbine and slipped the cartridges into his own magazine. He handed the knife to the telepath. 'Carry this. If you have to, use it.'

'There's another. Very faint, but I can hear him.'

'Where?'

'That way.' Taiyan flapped a hand toward the east. 'A little behind us.'

'We'll leave him,' decided Kennedy. 'You'll know if he tries to follow us; unless he does he's best left alone.'

'An enemy?'

'This place is full of them. If he lets out a yell or fires his gun they'll know just where we are. Now let's get moving. I want to reach the sanctuary before dark.'

He kept to his left, heading toward the area cleared by the elgets, halting as the observation tower came into sight. It was late afternoon and he was tempted to halt for the night, to use the cover of darkness to mask their final rush. But Taiyan couldn't last. The strength given by the food and water had gone, the fever induced by the poison in his leg burning up the last of his reserves. By morning, without medical aid, he would be dead.

Kennedy studied his map, irritated at the way his eyes confused detail; sweat, fatigue, and dehydration had combined to rob him of his fine edge. Days on Zarsh were long, the sun like a blowtorch, so what had to be done must be done soon.

He concentrated on the map, on the five black circles he had drawn with the tip of a bullet.

'Are you certain there are no others?' He turned to where the telepath lay sprawled on the rocky sand. *Taiyan, answer me, damn you!* He screamed the thought. *Are these all you can find?*

Taiyan spoke to the sky. 'That's all,' he whispered. 'Two are very faint. One is louder. Two are very close.'

Kennedy frowned. Apparently some of the hunters had guessed that the distraction caused by the escaping elgets was no accident. That or they had reached the conclusion the area offered a higher probability of success. He was, he remembered, up against professionals, men who earned their living by stalking game.

The map was of little help, but he had done his best to guess at the whereabouts of the hunters Tayan had spotted. He'd ignore the ones who were faint. The one a little closer could be avoided with luck. The others?

He leaned back, thinking. They had managed to get into one of the natural exits from the open ground, a relatively deep passage wending between tumbled boulders and leading directly toward sanctuary. It was an obvious place for patient hunters to wait, taking the chance that either the quarry or the man who had already collected the trophy would be coming that way. There would be other routes, but they also would be guarded, and the more they moved around the greater the chance they would be spotted.

He thought: *On your feet, Taiyan. It's time we were moving.*

'I can't.'

You can and you will! Kennedy used his mind like the lash of a whip. Thinking was safer than talking here where keen ears could pick up a reflected whisper. *Don't argue about it. Don't talk about it. Just do it. Up, damn you. Up!*

He watched as the telepath rolled over to hands and knees, and slowly lifted his body from the sand. Anger was a stimulant and he applied it with calculated deliberation.

Up, you weak-kneed freak! Get up and stand like a man. You want to die out here like a roasted animal? Move or I'll leave you to rot!

'Don't.' The telepath staggered to his feet. His eyes were wild, bright with fever. 'Loud,' he complained. 'You think too loud. You hurt my head when you shout like that.'

Kennedy whispered in his ear: 'Now listen. I'm going to take care of the opposition. Concentrate on my mind. When I give the signal you start walking. Don't waste any time and don't stop for any reason. You understand?'

'I think so.' Taiyan licked his cracked lips. 'Will it be far to go?'

'No. You can make it. Just think of all the water that is waiting for you. Gallons of it. Ice cold and sweet as sugar. Don't stop until you are on the blue sand. No matter what happens don't stop.'

'And you?'

'I'll be all right.' Kennedy gripped the thin shoulder, feeling the bones beneath his hand. 'Is there anything you want to add to what you've told me? Something you may have remembered?'

70

'About Merah?' Taiyan shook his head. 'I don't think so. No, wait. The building I told you about. It has cellars beneath. Ser Prome used to spend a lot of time in them.'

He had said that before, but Kennedy was patient. It could be his last chance to obtain information.

'Anything else?'

'He uses a lot of animals. Melots from Puko. I remember now. And the marshal isn't happy at what is happening. He wants to escape but can't. Luang won't let him. And I remember that once we had a party and there were some dancers and one of them liked the marshal and he gave her – ' Taiyan frowned. 'What did he give her? A jewel? A pet? No, he gave her a baton. That's right. A baton with a crest on the top. He said it would open every door on the planet. But it wasn't a key, so how could it open doors?'

He was rambling, on the edge of delirium, fantasies mixed in his mind. Gently Kennedy slapped him on the cheek.

'Snap out of it,' he whispered and then, using his mind as he dared not use his voice, shouted, *I'm going. Do as I told you. Quit dreaming and concentrate. You know what will happen if you don't.* He projected a mental picture of a body blasted with slugs, the neck a spouting fountain.

Taiyan shuddered.

Another picture of a head, the eyes open, a hand clutching the hair, blood streaming from the neck. Taiyan's head.

Yuah moaned. 'Please. I understand.'

Remember it!

Kennedy had done all he could. Anger and fear should drive the man on his way; if not, then he would die. Turning, Kennedy mounted a large boulder, crossed it, dropped to a shallow ravine. Beyond lay an almost sheer wall. He climbed it with the skill of long practice, rising to his feet as he cleared the edge. A jumble of close-packed stone made an uneven plateau running toward the slope leading to sanctuary. Kennedy walked openly, collar thrown open, the carbine held high in one hand, his other, empty, in plain view. On the exposed surface he couldn't be missed. He didn't want to be missed. He wanted to be spotted, recognized as an unsuccessful hunter, and allowed to get close to where he could locate and distract those waiting for the telepath.

It was a calculated gamble based on the assumed reluctance

of a civilized man to kill one of his own kind.

A gamble he almost lost.

The first shot came as he reached a shallow gully. There was a hard, flat sound, and something slammed into his side, spinning him backward and down. He rolled as a second shot chipped stone inches from his face, dropping into the gully. Safe in cover, he shouldered his carbine and waited.

The hunter was overconfident. He appeared over the edge, a black silhouette against the sky, head craned forward as he searched for his victim. He caught a glimpse of Kennedy's foot, the bright crimson of blood on the rock, and yelled his triumph.

'I've got him! Here! He's mine!'

He was still shouting when Kennedy shot him through the mouth.

Move! he thought. Taiyan, move!

He fired again, twice more into the air, then looked down at his side. The bullet had ripped through the hard muscle at the left side of his waist. The wound wasn't serious, but blood streamed from the twin punctures to run down his leg and puddle on the ground at his feet. Setting aside his carbine, Kennedy stripped the shirt and belt from the dead hunter. Wadding the shirt, he strapped it tight against the wound. As he reached for the carbine, a foot kicked it away.

'You won't need that,' said Chon Selman.

He had approached with the stealth of a cat, his boots soundless on the rock, not even a shadow betraying his presence. A man perfectly at home in the savage environment. Kennedy straightened, meeting the hunter's eyes, seeing the carbine he held aimed at his heart.

Quietly he said, 'Are you going to finish what your friend started?'

'He's no friend of mine.'

'I'm glad to hear it. He tried to murder me. If you have the same idea you should have shot me from behind.'

'Murder?'

'What else? He knew that I wasn't the quarry. He could see my gun, my bare throat, and I walked in the open. Would the quarry have done that? Shown himself in plain sight?'

'He might,' said the hunter. 'If he was clever he could have downed a hunter, taken his clothes and weapons, and decided on a bluff.'

72

'And his collar?' Kennedy glanced at the dead man. 'He knew what he was doing. That yell was for your benefit, so that he could later claim to have made a genuine mistake.'

Selman shrugged. 'There was no need of that. In the open ground anything goes. You were just competition to be eliminated.' His carbine lifted a little. 'You still are competition.'

Taiyan! Move! Move! Aloud Kennedy said, 'Did Aihun Zemao offer you a bonus to kill me?'

'I'm no assassin.'

'No? You could have fooled me.' Kennedy gestured toward his carbine, talking for the sake of it, holding the man's attention. 'That's empty. You heard me fire three times. Even if I had it in my hand and you fired it would still be murder. The open ground,' he added bitterly. 'A nice place. Just the spot for real, red-blooded heroes.'

'You dislike our ways?'

'I think they stink,' said Kennedy deliberately. 'You give your quarry no chance at all. They come out practically naked, unarmed, and all you sportsmen have to do is to sit and wait to bring them down. The one you're after now, for example. Has he got a gun? A knife? And you claim that you aren't an assassin. One day, maybe, I'll appreciate the difference.'

For a moment Selman faced him, fighting his rage, then slowly he lowered his weapon. For some reason he felt the need to explain, to gain this man's understanding and perhaps respect.

'There is a difference,' he said. 'For me at least. And you're wrong about the quarry being helpless. He is a man with a reasoning brain and that makes him dangerous. He could find arms; the loincloth would make a sling, for example, and a thrown stone can be as effective as a bullet. No,' he snapped, as Kennedy reached for the carbine. 'Don't touch it.'

'It's empty.'

'Maybe, but that's an old trick. You could have won extra ammunition.'

Clever, thought Kennedy. The hunter was no stranger to the open ground, but perhaps not clever enough. While he talked Taiyan was moving toward safety. Yet how could Selman suspect that the quarry had a friend? Kennedy watched as Selman picked up the weapon and ejected the cartridges. A sign, at least, that the hunter did not intend to kill him. Had he wanted to shoot he would have done so by now.

He said casually, 'Where is Aihun Zemao?'

'Waiting.' Selman anticipated what he assumed would be the next question. 'Don't ask me to work against him. You are a stranger and would not understand the ethics of the hunt, as you do not appreciate the danger of a quarry. You – ' He broke off, eyes widening. 'The quarry!'

He turned, leaping up to the edge of the gully. A high boulder lay a little ahead and he ran to the summit. Kennedy chased after him. There was no time to search for the dead hunter's carbine, it had fallen beneath his body, but he still retained his knife. It flashed in the sun as he ran to where Selman stood.

Ahead, beyond the torn rock of the open ground, Yuan Taiyan staggered toward the blue sand.

'No!' Kennedy shouted as the hunter raised his carbine. He was too far to deflect the weapon and the man couldn't possibly miss. Kennedy swung his arm, the knife a glittering arc as it spun through the air, the blade ringing as it struck the barrel as Selman fired.

The bullet missed and Kennedy gave him no chance to fire again. Selman grunted as he turned, the stiffened edge of Kennedy's hand missing the side of the neck and landing with numbing force against the bicep. The carbine fell from the hunter's grip and he snatched at his knife with his good arm.

'You!' he spat. 'The quarry! Working together!'

The knife swung upward in a stomach-ripping slash.

Kennedy dodged it, caught the wrist as it rose, and twisted with savage force. He could have snapped the bone; instead he wrenched flesh and muscle, strained tendons and sinew. The knife fell, Selman following, jerked off balance to fall heavily on the rock.

'You fool!' he panted. 'You – '

They both heard the sound of the shot.

Kennedy turned, staring ahead at the small figure so close to safety, at Aihun Zemao crouched behind a rock, his carbine leveled. The first shot had missed, but the second hit. Taiyan staggered and fell, rising to lunge desperately ahead, blood bright on his back and shoulder.

'No!' yelled Selman. 'Don't!'

If the Merahinian heard him he ignored the call. The quarry was almost safe and if he lived, there would be questions to

74

answer, the penalty of failure to be paid. Carefully Zemao aimed and gently squeezed the trigger. The bullet went true, slamming into Taiyan's spine, hurling him forward as it took his life, sending him over the line to sprawl on the blue sand.

CHAPTER ELEVEN

'Poetic justice,' said Luden. 'Sometimes it happens and, when it does, I must confess to a certain degree of pleasure. Aihun Zemao should have listened to his hunter's warning. If he had he would not be in prison now. And, as Yuah Taiyan had been committed for life, he will be there for a long time. Unless,' he added musingly, 'he decides to volunteer for quarry.'

'He won't,' said Kennedy. 'But if he does, maybe I'll pay another visit to Zarsh.'

'Not without me, you won't,' rumbled Penza Saratov. 'You almost got killed there, Cap. You took too many chances. Now let me look at that wound.'

Kennedy relaxed as the giant probed at his side. Around him the *Mordain* hummed with quiet efficiency and an attractive odor came from the galley where Chemile was brewing coffee. As Saratov finished his ministrations Chemile appeared with steaming cups.

'My best,' he announced. 'I roasted the beans myself and ground them just right.' He watched as Kennedy sipped. 'Good, Cap?'

'Very good, Veem.'

Chemile grinned. 'I thought you'd say that. Penza would, too, only he's too jealous to pay me a compliment. He forgets at times that strength isn't everything. I mean, could he have sneaked in that ranch and set those devices? He would have been spotted right away.'

'Who made them?' demanded the giant.

'You did,' admitted Chemile. 'With Jarl's help, but any good mechanic could have done the same.'

'And any dishwasher in any cheap restaurant could make better coffee than you can,' stormed the giant. 'This stuff isn't fit to wash down the paint.'

'If you don't like it you know what you can do,' said Chemile stiffly. 'An artist like myself doesn't have to bandy words with a common engineer. I don't have to make you coffee. Right, Cap?'

'Right,' agreed Kennedy. 'But what about the rest of us? Jarl likes your coffee and so do I. You wouldn't want us to suffer because of Penza's lack of appreciation.'

'He's under strain,' added Luden shrewdly. 'You know how Penza is when he can't take a part in the action. He was restless all the time you were at the ranch. I wouldn't mind taking a small bet that he's sorry for what he said.'

Chemile smirked. 'Well, if he's willing to apologize, then – '

'Apologize to you, you freak?' Saratov's voice boomed from the bulkheads. 'I'll walk space without a suit first!'

'Veem, you'd do better to take over the bridge,' said Kennedy hastily. With the *Mordain* on full automatic control it wasn't strictly necessary, but it would serve to end the argument. At times he found the good-natured bickering between the pair a little tiring. 'Penza, could you make a few very small broadcasters? I want some units about the size of a pea, self-powered, which will each send out a different signal. About five will do.'

'Sure, Cap. Range?'

'A few miles. Hit an optimum size-weight operational ratio.'

Penza frowned. 'I can do it, Cap, but it would help if you let me know just how they are to be used.'

'I want to introduce them into the physical structure of a small animal. They could be swallowed, but I don't want them to be eliminated as waste. Operating time?' Kennedy paused, thinking. 'Say about eight days. We'll need a detector as well, of course.'

As the giant bustled away Luden said, 'You have a plan, Cap?'

'Call it a means of verification. Yuah Taiyan told me all he knew about the Chambodians' base. The trouble is that while he could tell me what he saw, he couldn't tell me exactly where he saw it.' Kennedy led the way into the chart room where maps of Merah, received by hybeam from Commander Avery of MALACA 9, lay scattered on the table. 'We can assume that it lies somewhere near the capital,' he said. 'At least Yua Taiyan had that impression, though he had no idea as to the actual distance. There was a river running in a wide loop at the center of which lay a long, low building. Three rivers run into the capital and each has many loops. See?'

Luden followed the pointing finger. 'Was there more, Cap?'

'The building has cellars and a flat, central roof with eaves which sweep up and outward like those of a pagoda.'

'The cellars will be invisible and the roof will follow the usual pattern of Merahinian architecture,' said Luden. 'Not a great deal of help, Cap. Did he describe the surroundings?'

'Close-cut grass sweeping to the river, some flower beds, a landing place nearby for heavy-duty copters. The river has a small wharf and, at times, he saw a boat. It lay to the north of the capital, which at least eliminates one of the rivers.' Kennedy remembered Taiyan's loss of orientation. 'At least it would if we could rely on his judgement. He wasn't even sure about the distance; though, of course, whoever took him there could have used a circular route in order to deceive him.'

'A natural precaution.' Luden brooded over the map. 'There must be hundreds of riverside buildings in an area, say, within a hundred miles of the city. And, naturally, the structure will have been made to appear innocuous. We can find it, but it will take a great deal of time.'

'Which is why I'm having Penza make those units. The laboratory uses animals, melots from Puko. They could guide us to where we want to go.'

Luden was thoughtful. 'Melots,' he murmured. 'I recall a paper written about them by Savant Deasel of the University of Puko. They apparently have a conscious control of subconscious influence. In the wild state they live in communities similar to the baboons of Earth. As pets they are amazingly docile and yet, at times, show extremes of violent emotion. Deasel's conclusions were that they had, in some manner, control over the censors in their minds – a thing unusual for any animal. He hinted that they could represent the members of a race on the edge of achieving logical thought and reason. It could be that the Chambodian is interested in them for that reason.'

Luden reasoned that an extract taken from the tissues of their brains, or a secretion of their ductless glands, could have given the Chambodian the secret of nullifying the one thing which kept men from turning into beasts. In that case there would be a constant demand for the animals to be delivered to the hidden laboratory.

Luden said, 'The units, Cap. Do you hope to introduce them into the physical structure of the creatures so they will guide us to Ser Prome's installation?'

'That's right, Jarl.'

'But how are you going to find a consignment heading for Merah?' Luden shook his head before Kennedy could answer, irritated at himself for his slowness of thought. 'Of course! Commander Avery of MALACA Nine.'

He was a big man with a hawk-face and eyes which were creased with a multitude of tiny lines. He looked out from the screen, impeccable in his uniform of green and blue edged with silver, then dropped his eyes to read the papers before him.

'You're lucky, Cap,' Avery said. 'There's a consignment heading your way for Merah. A load of melots from Vorot.'

'Vorot?'

'That's right, Cap. A mysterious buyer cleared out the entire stock of a breeding farm there. Puko limits the export of the beasts, both to maintain the price and to conserve the stock, so whoever went shopping had to take what he could get. The ship is the *Elget*, Captain Baker in command. If you want to intercept them you'll have to move fast.'

'Coordinates?'

Kennedy frowned as Avery gave them. It would be close. To Luden he said, 'Tell Veem to alter course and apply full power. I want to approach the *Elget* from the direction of Merah, but far enough out to avoid their patrols.'

Avery said, 'Will you need help, Cap?'

'As yet, no.'

'A pity.' The commander sighed. 'My boys are spoiling for action. I've had a dozen requests for transfers in the past month and every last one of them wants to become a Free Acting Terran Envoy. They seem to think that once accepted they will live lives of glamorous ease. Maybe you should pay us a visit and do a little reeducating.'

Kennedy smiled. 'Show them my scars, you mean?'

'Something like that. None of them will make it, of course. They're good men, but nowhere near the class of FATE. I'm giving them a taste of preliminary training and adjusting their viewpoint. But I can't blame them. At times I wish I could get out of this chair and get into action myself.' Avery sighed again. 'Well, that's the way it goes. Luck, Cap.'

Kennedy turned as the screen went dark. Around him the *Mordain* quivered as it plunged through hyspace at the full extent of its power. At his bench Penza scowled as his big hands constructed tiny mechanisms. Back at the chart table Kennedy pushed aside the maps and studied a sheet of various uniforms. That of the Merahinian space patrol occupied his full attention.

'A major,' he decided. 'A rank high enough to command respectful obedience and yet not too high so as to arouse suspicion. How are you at tailoring, Jarl?'

Luden sighed; he had been through this before. Stiffly he said, 'It isn't one of my best accomplishments, Cap, but I will do what I can.'

'I know that, Jarl.'

'How many uniforms will you need?'

'Just the one. Chemile can plant the units while you and Penza handle the *Mordain*.' Kennedy reached for rolls of colored fabric and plastic. 'We haven't much time. I want to reach the *Elget* as far from Merah as possible. It might be awkward if we bumped into a genuine patrol.'

They were lucky. On the screens the shape of the *Elget* was alone and no other vessel revealed itself on the detectors. Captain Baker was a hard, rough man, typical of the traders who roved between the stars taking a profit where they could, willing to accept any charter or cargo if the price was right.

He said, 'What the hell is this? I'm a genuine carrier minding my own business.'

'You are approaching Merah,' snapped Kennedy. He wore the uniform Luden had made, his face hard beneath the visored cap. 'Prepare for inspection. We will match speed to make connection. If you break it or alter course or velocity you will be instantly destroyed.'

Baker scowled and looked at something beyond the range of the scanners. Kennedy could see the interior of the vessel on the communicator screen beyond Baker's image. It matched its captain – harsh, bleak, bare metal, and stained paint. Crew and maintenance cost money which Baker didn't have. But he had been through all this many times in the past. He shrugged with resignation.

'All right,' he said. 'I'm clean. Come aboard when ready.'

A short tube connected both air-locks, providing safe passage through the void. Kennedy marched through it to where the captain stood. Ignoring the outstretched hand, he snapped, 'Your cargo manifest?'

'Here.' Baker handed over a soiled sheet of paper. 'Nothing special. Just some perfume in bulk, a few mutated seeds, a little spice, and a load of animals.'

'Animals?'

'Melots.' His scowl deepened. 'Say, what's this all about? I've been to Merah lots of times before and never been boarded once. The port inspection's always been enough.'

'We have reason to believe that contraband is being smuggled to the planet.' Kennedy handed back the manifest. 'Who ordered the animals?'

'How the hell would I know? I just carry them.'

'To be collected at the spacefield?' One hope had gone, there was no notification of final destination, but Kennedy hadn't expected any. It was an elementary precaution for the Chambodian to have taken.

'That's right. What's wrong with that?'

'Nothing. How many in the crew?'

The number Baker quoted was too low for a vessel of this size and with a living cargo, but Kennedy made no comment. Tall, arrogant, his voice carrying the snap of command, Kennedy maintained the pretense of official inspection. Chemile would be in the vessel by now, blending into the background, the small case he carried safely hidden behind his back. But he had to be given access to the melots.

They were in the hold, caged in serried ranks, eyes bright and wary as they saw the visitors. Kennedy paused at the door, nose wrinkling at the scent. It was a heavy musk combined with other stenches, the product of lack of cleaning and care.

Curtly he said, 'You keep a foul ship, Captain.'

'Not good enough for you bright boys in uniform?'

'Not good enough for any civilized man or planet,' snapped Kennedy. 'Merah isn't a garbage dump for you to get rid of your trash. I've half a mind to condemn this vessel. Perhaps you'd better spend five days in quarantine just in case you're carrying something we could do without.'

'Now listen – '

'I am a major! You will address me as such! One more

6   81

example of disrespect to my uniform and I shall place you and your vessel under restraint!'

There was no doubt he meant it. Baker swallowed, visualizing endless delays and loss of income. His ship could be fined, himself made bankrupt, imprisoned even. And Merah was not a gentle world to those who fell foul of its laws.

'I'm sorry, Major,' he said. 'I do my best, but I'm shorthanded, and you know how things are when you're carrying livestock. But the ship's clean as regards contraband.'

'So you say. I would hardly expect you to say otherwise. I think that a thorough search and decontamination might be called for.'

Baker caught the doubt and fought to restrain his anger. Smoothly he said, 'I don't think there's need for that, sir. If you'd like to come back to the control room we could talk about it. In the meantime I'll get a man to clean up in here.'

'Later.' Kennedy wanted no witnesses to Chemile's activity. He sniffed again and turned toward the door. 'This stench is appalling. Where is your log?'

'In the control room,' Baker snapped, then added, carefully, 'Do you want to inspect it, sir?'

Alone Chemile breathed a sigh of relief. The door to the cargo hold had been left ajar; he stepped from the hull against which he had blended, crossed to it, and looked through the gap. No one was in sight. Turning toward the cages he opened the small case Penza had given him. Inside, resting on plastic foam, lay five ovoid nodules.

Selecting one, he held it through the bars of the nearest cage.

'Here, boy,' he whispered. 'Have yourself a treat.'

The melot stared back with glassy eyes.

It was a cross between a monkey and a bear, a small, compact body with furred legs and arms, the hand fitted with an opposing thumb. The head was round, long-nosed, the ears pointed and tufted. A ringed tail lay coiled on the floor of the cage. A fully grown specimen, standing, was about three feet tall. As laboratory subjects they were in great demand as their metabolism was close to that of a man. As pets they could be trained to fetch and carry, to stand guard and to give the alarm in case of fire or intruders. Their intelligence was about twice that of a dog.

'Here,' urged Chemile. 'Take it. It's nice.'

A paw lifted and grasped the ovoid, holding it close to the nose. The unit itself was little larger than a pea covered with thin, hooked spines, the whole coated with a sweet substance. As Chemile watched the melot licked it, thrust it into its mouth, and swallowed.

'Good boy.'

Chemile moved to another cage. The sweet coating would dissolve, the thin spines hook into the intestine, and the stomach accids would induce the broadcast powered by the interaction of dissolving alloys. In eight days the entire unit would have vanished without harm or discomfort to the animal.

As he fed the last of the units to a melot, the door to the hold slammed open.

Chemile froze, standing hard against the hull, his skin taking on the flaked and scaled appearance of the metal. Two men entered the hold. One of them leaned against the cages, chewing, the blue of keel juice edging his lips.

'A hell of a job,' he complained. 'I'm supposed to be the engineer, but instead I'm a damned nursemaid to a bunch of animals. What's got into Baker? He was never so particular before. Hell, before you know it, he'll have us scrubbing the decks and repainting the hull.'

'Go through the motions,' advised his companion. 'While that snotty major is around we've got to put on a show.'

'And that's something else. We've never been stopped before. Do you think the old man's up to something? Making a little profit on the side, maybe?'

'I doubt it.'

'It could be that,' insisted the man. He spat, blue juice adding fresh stains to the floor. 'I don't trust him. This is a commune vessel, we share the profits, but if he's doing a little private trading I want to know about it. And, if you''re smart, Blen, you'll want to know too.'

'I know enough to mind my own business,' snapped Blen. 'And keep your voice down. If that major gets suspicious we'll all wind up in jail. All right, let's get started. You take this end while I take the other.'

Chemile was worried. If he moved and was spotted the entire operation would be ruined; yet he had to get out and back to the *Mordain*. As the man passed him he moved, stepping toward the rank of cages near to the door, freezing as Blen's companion spun, his eyes suspicious.

'What was that?'

Blen scowled. 'What was what?'

'I saw something move.'

'Of course you did. The animals are restless. They probably want feeding.'

'Not an animal.' The man roved between the cages. 'It was big, like a man.'

'In here?' Blen snorted his disgust. 'Where would he be hiding? You must be going crazy. That stuff you chew is blasting your mind.'

It could be true; keel was an insidious chewing weed which brought first euphoria, then insanity leading to death. Hallucinations were common toward the final stages. The man wiped at his mouth and looked at the blue stain.

'I – ' he swallowed. 'I saw it,' he insisted. 'A reflection. I'm sure I saw it.'

'Look around,' snapped Blen impatiently. 'Can you see it now? No, so it can't be here, can it? If it was I'd see it. Now get over here and help clean up this mess.'

Chemile slipped through the door as the man obeyed, moving quickly as their backs turned toward him. He froze again at the entrance to the control room. Kennedy was facing Baker, who stood with his back toward the air-lock. No one else was in sight.

As Chemile dived into the lock Kennedy said, 'Well, Captain, I think that I can permit you to continue your journey. However, I would advise you to take a less truculent attitude should you be challenged again. My compatriots are not as understanding as myself. Were you challenged before I made contact?'

'No, sir. We had a clear run from Vorot.' Baker felt a sense of relief. He hadn't dared to try outright bribery, but he had fed the officer some of his best wine and had almost groveled at his feet. Both were hard things to do for a man of his temperament.

'That's just as well,' said Kennedy blandly. 'If you had I would have had no choice but to place you under restraint for interrogation. The state of your vessel and the possibility of bribery, you understand. There is no need to elaborate, I'm sure.'

'No,' said Baker hastily. 'I understand.'

Back in the *Mordain* Kennedy watched as the ships drifted apart, the *Elget* heading directly toward Merah. If stopped Baker wouldn't mention the present encounter; certainly he wouldn't report it. All he would want to do would be to get unloaded, get paid, and be on his way.

From his bench Saratov called, 'Signals coming through, Cap.'

They would fade as the ships parted, dying as the distance increased, but later, on Merah, they could be picked up and, Kennedy hoped, guide them to the secret laboratory. He hoped they'd lead to the place where the mind-death was made and which threatened the very existence of Earth itself. A place and a secret which had to be destroyed no matter what the cost.

CHAPTER TWELVE

Kota Bassein reached the end of the room, turned, paced back down the length of the chamber. Around him hung paintings made of gems set in precious metals, winking points of ruby and emerald, of topaz and sapphire, the smolder of opal, the iridescence of zavorite. From pendants hung chiming gongs, and fretted glass made an enticing distraction. He noted none of them, pacing, brooding, his face set in heavy lines.

'You are disturbed, my lord.'

The girl on the couch was lissome, her body lithe, soft fabrics and worked metal ornaments accentuating her curves. Her hair was a cloud in which glowed minute stars and the scent of her perfume hovered like incense around the perfection of her face.

A stringed instrument rested beside her. She picked it up and plucked a chord. It hung for a moment as if suspended in the air to fade and die with murmurings from the hanging chimes.

'Does Gydia no longer please you, my lord?'

The talk of the seraglio, but Bassein was in no mood for it now. He had not been in the mood for how long? He knew the date to an hour. Since the time he had watched men and women kill each other like ravening beasts. The time when guards had come to slaughter them like the animals they had become.

A marshal of Merah should have greater strength.

Again his feet pounded the carpet. Ipoh Luang would have no such thoughts, and he could think of none of the cabal who shared his disquiet. They were young fools who had yet to learn the danger of underestimating an enemy. They boasted in the privacy of their chambers of how easy it would be to raid the Terran Sphere. Arguing how to share the spoils of a defeated Earth. And the Chambodian didn't help. Always he was there with his cold determination, his hints, his words, his subtle innuendos. Ser Prome, an enemy in the guise of a friend and

86

benefactor. Why couldn't the others see what was so plain?

'My lord?' The girl was anxious. 'Sit and let me play to you. An air from Salekard which I learned long ago.' The instrument in her hands thrummed as she touched the strings with fingers as delicate as lace.

'No.' He was in no mood for music.

'Wine then, my lord?'

'No.'

'Would you care to watch me dance?' A control yielded beneath her hand and the erotic pulse of Kasendian rhythms filled the air. She rose, weaving in time, every gesture an alluring invitation. 'My lord?'

He watched, conscious of her expert control of every muscle of her body, the arduous training which had made her what she was. A joy to be savored by those who could afford the price. And yet the dance had no more effect than all her other blandishments and she was quick to recognize it.

She killed the music and, in the following silence said, 'You are tired, my lord.'

She meant old but knew better than to say it. If she had she would have carried the mark of his displeasure on her face until the hour of her death.

'Tired,' she repeated softly. 'Come and rest for a while in the comfort of my arms. Sleep and wake a man refreshed by sweet dreams and pleasant ease.'

For a moment he was tempted, then shook his head. It had been a mistake to come to this place, but the fault was minor and could quickly be forgotten. He had hoped to find surcease of mental strain and instead had found only hated images. Softness and beauty compared to savage violence. What would she turn into, he wondered, if a certain substance were to be slipped into her wine? How vicious was the devil which would be released? He tried to imagine her hands tipped with blood, the eyes wide, staring, the mouth slavering with rage. She had been taught to love; had every lesson been accompanied by the urge to hate?

'My lord!' She had seen the expression on his face and with quick intuition took steps to safeguard her position. 'I have offended you. How can I make amends?'

By talking, he thought. By matching his worries and concerns and appreciating his fears. But that was impossible. At all costs the secret had to be kept, and even the walls of a seraglio had ears.

'You have not offended me,' he said gently. 'There is no need to make amends.'

'You are more than kind, my lord.' Her eyes widened as he reached for his cap. 'You are leaving so soon?'

There was no point in staying. She belonged to the past, a time when he had carried no crushing burden of worry and doubt. As a toy she was superb, but now he had no time for toys, and yet he could be kind.

'You will suffer no loss,' he promised. 'There will be no talk of failure. And, perhaps, some other time – '

He left the promise hanging as he headed toward the door.

His personal flier stood on the roof. The pilot, a grim, taciturn veteran, glanced once at the marshal's face, then stared at his controls. It was no time for comment, no matter how favored his position.

'Up,' ordered Bassein. 'Circle the city.'

Broodingly he stared below at the streets and houses, and the purposeful crowds. Uniforms were everywhere; even at this height he could sense the martial fever which had gripped the town. It had been deliberately fostered by the experts of propaganda, accentuating the normal military atmosphere of the planet. For it had been necessary to have a military regime. A newly settled world needed a strong directive hand and a government dedicated to survival. But Bassein thought that time had passed and perhaps the regime had lasted too long.

Traitorous thoughts, he knew, and ones which would be severely punished if voiced by one of lesser rank. And even he dared not voice them openly to others of the cabal.

To the pilot he said, 'Contact Ipoh Luang. Personal connection.'

His aide had been engaged on mysterious business lately and it would be well to keep a check on his whereabouts. With intrigue thick in the air no man could regard himself as safe.

'No success, sir.' The pilot spoke without turning his head. 'He left the office leaving no word as to his destination.'

'Get me the laboratory.'

Ser Prome came on the screen, his bird-face expressionless as ever. 'Marshal?'

'Is Ipoh Luang with you?'

'Yes.'

'For any special reason?'

'He is taking an interest in my progress. As you know, production of the drug has been hampered by the lack of suitable animals. We now have a new supply and I am treating them. More important, I am trying to synthesize the essential ingredient which forms the basis of the substance you know. May I remark that I consider this communication to be unwise. You are the marshal of Merah and it is possible that certain interested parties are taking a special note of what you do and say at this time.'

Bassein made a tremendous effort to control his rage. Thickly he said, 'You forget yourself, Chambodian.'

'I, Marshal? I think not. I work for Merah.'

'And I do not?'

'I have no opinion on that matter. Even so it would be best to allow things to follow their own course. And now, if you will excuse me, there are matters needing my attention.'

It was inconceivable that the rudeness could be accidental. Luang had gone out to the laboratory and others could be with him, plotting, perhaps, against Bassein. The Chambodian, with typical calculation, had chosen sides, perhaps while he, Bassein, wasted time in stupid dalliance. And, now that he came to think of it, he had visited the seraglio at Luang's suggestion. For a long moment Bassein stared at the blank screen, fighting his anger, striving for coolness. Now, as never before, he must plan before acting.

The laboartory was the key. Win it and the others would come to heel.

'To the barracks,' he ordered the pilot. 'I want twenty men you can trust. Two copters and see that every man is fully armed.'

'I shall need authority, sir.'

'You have it. I shall be in command.' Bassein noted the man's hesitation and snapped: 'What is the matter? You think to disobey?'

'Not me, sir. I was thinking. There is a detachment of guards at the field near Chomba. A unit of the training cadre. We could take the entire group together with equipment. Thirty men with transports. If we go to the barracks it will be hard to keep things secret. I assume, sir, that you don't want more people than necessary to know about this.'

Did the pilot know what was going on? If he did and had sided with Luang then Bassein was as good as dead. Bassein decided to take the chance. If he was to act it had to be immediately.

'We'll do as you suggest. Complete secrecy now and at all times. Orders will be given en route. You understand?'

Like his pilot the men were hardened veterans used to weapons and trained to obey without question. Bassein watched as they filed into two copters and took to the air following his own flier. He began to feel a heady euphoria as he had when first donning uniform. This was the true reward of military service. Not the regular food, the calculated adulation, the espirit de corps so painstakingly cultivated, but the sweep and flow of action. Without it life was dull with sickening monotony. Men trained to use the weapons and violence could only grow stale and irritable unless their skills were employed.

As they neared the laboratory he said into the communicator:

'Listen. It is the marshal of Merah who speaks. You are under my direct command. We are approaching a building which contains treasonable elements. It is to be taken without hesitation. If any resist they are to be eliminated at once. Do no damage. Kill none who show no signs of opposition. I am watching. Do a good job and you will all be rewarded with a higher rank. Fail and you will pay the penalty.' He paused, then added, 'What you do is for the good of Merah. You fight for peace, stability, and the safety of the planet. Officers, report under private communication.'

Two faces appeared on the split screen.

'Lieutenant Chrodai, sir. First transport.'

'Captain Wee, sir. Second transport.'

'Lieutenant, you will land on the roof and immediately make an entrance into the interior. Captain, as he lands you will hit ground and ring the building. Move in at once and effect entry from the ground level. Take and hold prisoner all personnel. Remember my instructions and kill no more than is essential. Both of you, there is a Chambodian inside. He is not to be hurt under any circumstances. No further communication. Out!'

It was a neat, simple plan and should have worked. Those within had no reason to expect a sudden attack and would not be on the defensive. The normal guards would be instantly overwhelmed. A textbook exercise of skillfully applied force with a predictable result.

Only it didn't happen like that.

Bassein watched from his flier as the two transports moved into position. It was late afternoon, the sun throwing long shadows and turning the river into a loop of crimson fire. As the lieutenant dropped toward the roof more fire spouted from an open trap in the concrete, a shaft of vivid flame, the focused beam of raw energy hitting the copter, slicing it in half, sending molten rain dripping to join the shattered fabric and tumbling men.

'A Dione!' The pilot turned, his face startled. 'They blasted that plane with a Dione.'

The roar of the discharge echoed his words. It came again, twice more, the gun rising on its platform to bathe the roof with searing destruction, crisping bodies into ash, blasting the remains of the transport to slag.

On the ground the captain met with a similar fate. As the skids touched a panel opened in the wall of the building and a stream of missiles ripped into the fuselage venting their energy into gouting explosions, tearing flesh and bone into minced shreds.

From the roof the Dione fired again, completing the total destruction of the attacking force.

'Quick!' Bassein recovered from his shocked paralysis. 'Up and away. Fast!'

A trap, he thought bitterly, and he had walked into it like a fool. The calculated rudeness of the Chambodian, Luang's absence, all bait to make him come running. And, knowing him, they would have guessed that he would come with men and weapons to counteract the supposed coup. Instead he had committed an outright act of treason.

'Up!' he snapped again. 'Away!'

There was still a thin chance. Get to the barracks, assemble more men, get his story in first to the cabal; when Luang and the others were dead he would still retain command. And, if he totally destroyed the laboratory, it would solve more problems than one.

He had left it too late. As the flier fought to gain altitude the muzzle of the Dione lifted, aimed, spat a shaft of flame. The pilot cried out as the tail vanished in incandescent fury, then fell silent as he struggled to control the falling mass of metal. The rotors broke their fall, the crippled vessel slamming into the dirt of a flower bed.

Shaken, Bassein struggled from the rear compartment. The pilot was dead, his head crushed and neck broken, blind eyes staring from the ruined face. Ahead lay the river, but before Bassein could reach it he was surrounded by armed men.

Luang was acidly polite. 'A regrettable occurrence, Marshal. In fact one almost impossible to comprehend. An act of blatant treachery against the state. For an officer of high rank to suborn military personnel to attack a government installation proves, surely, that he is either in the pay of an enemy power or has gone completely insane.'

Bassein said coldly, 'There is an alternative explanation, and one which I will be happy to expound to the cabal.'

'No doubt you would, but, unfortunately – ' Luang broke off, looking to where men worked to clear away the debris and the dead. 'A pity that you survived. However, it is obvious that you have suffered grave internal injuries and it is doubtful if you will live to see another dawn.'

'You intend to kill me?'

'My dear Marshal, I am being kind. Surely you do not wish for a full-dress court-martial during which your perfidity will be fully exposed? You have pride, and come from a respected family and, in any event, the outcome of a trial would be the same. What you have done merits death. Does it matter to you how it comes?'

He hates me, thought Bassein, looking at the smiling face. *He is enjoying this. Now he holds the upper hand and is tasting the sweetness of power, playing at cat and mouse, savoring the moment.*

He said, 'I demand a trial. As marshal of Merah I am entitled to a hearing.'

'You will get no trial.' No trial and no chance of warning Terra of the hell which was brewing in the laboratory. No chance either of warning the cautious among the cabal of the danger they faced, the threat of assassination which would eliminate all who opposed the dream of interstellar conquest. Luang added meaningfully, 'But you will get a hearing, Marshal. That I promise you. You will talk long and loud before you succumb to your injuries.'

CHAPTER THIRTEEN

Kennedy lowered the binoculars and palmed his burning eyes. Together with Saratov he lay prone on the brow of a low hill screened by a clump of trees, almost a mile from the laboratory and as close as he could safely get. Chemile and Luden were with the flier two miles to their rear. The professor was busy collecting botanical specimens for a supposed work on the local flora, a disguise which should pass casual inspection.

Saratov said, 'Hell, Cap, those boys play rough.' He too had watched the action through powerful lenses. 'A Dione on the roof, guns in the walls, guards by the dozen – that place is built like a fortress.'

'You're certain it's the place?'

'No mistake about it, Cap. Every one of those melots was taken there. The signals are plain. Does it look as Taiyan described?'

Kennedy nodded. 'He didn't know about the armament, but there was no reason why he should. And it's safe to guess that the entire grounds around the building must be fitted with electronic warning devices. The river, perhaps?' He lifted the binoculars and studied the loop again. 'I don't know,' he said finally. 'We're too far to be certain. It might be possible to get to the wharf, but from then on it would be a matter of risking traps and alarms. We'll have to think about this.'

Back at the flier Luden pursed his lips as he heard the report. 'It's obvious, Cap, there's been a military coup. It's inevitable in any rigid society where the only path to supreme power is by pulling down those above and climbing up on those below. Which means, of course, that the laboratory is a key factor. Verification of what we already know, but unfortunately it doesn't help us. Those inside now will be more than ever on their guard, so a direct frontal attack is out of the question.'

Chemile said, 'Couldn't we sneak in somehow? If they opened the door maybe I could get inside.'

'Simple,' said the giant impatiently. 'What do we do, just go up and knock?'

'Why not? You could wear uniforms and pretend it was an official matter. Just get that door open and –'

'A Trojan Horse,' interrupted Luden. 'Veem's right; it's the only way it could be done.'

Saratov blinked. 'A Trojan Horse?'

'A part of ancient Greek history. Troy was besieged, but the attacking army couldn't penetrate the walls. So they built a giant wooden horse, filled it with men, and left it behind as they sailed away. The Trojans took it inside the city as spoils of war. That night the men inside crept out and opened the city gates allowing the Greeks who had returned under cover of darkness to get inside.' Luden frowned, thinking. 'Now, how could we apply that precept to this particular situation? A military flier would be allowed to land, but in that case previous communication would have been established. And what reason could we give for demanding entry? I must confess that, at the moment, the solution to the problem eludes me.'

'But not me,' said Kennedy. 'Veem, take us back to the space-field. I'll explain as we go.'

There was a sense of unease in the city, accentuated by the coming of night so that the guard at the barracks was jumpy with nervous irritation. He snapped to a salute as a tall figure marched toward him, halting as he returned the salute. The tall man was a major, the guard judged as he noted the insignia on his collar, and a martinet judging by the hard look on his face and eyes. A civilian was with him, a man obscenely fat, dressed in loose garments and obviously terrified.

Kennedy, in the major's garb, snapped, 'Turn out the guard!'

Unthinking obedience was ingrained in all lower ranks. The guard obeyed, standing rigid as others poured from the guard-room to stand in line.

'Your commander?' Kennedy nodded as a noncom stepped forward. 'Detail two men to escort and take me directly to the highest officer present. Move!'

The officer was a colonel, very conscious of his rank, uneasy when faced with the unexpected. He glanced curiously at

Saratov, returned Kennedy's salute, and, as the escort left, said, 'What is all this about, Major?'

'A matter of the highest importance, sir. I have discovered a spy. This man' – he gestured toward Saratov – 'was discovered manipulating an electronic detection device of some kind. A signal is being emitted from a particular location and I think that it could be a message sent by the agent of an unfriendly power. In view of the present situation I need hardly stress the implications. Action, of course, must be taken at once.'

The colonel hesitated. 'Are you connected with Security, Major?'

That could be quickly checked. 'No, sir. I am a communications specialist. I was checking equipment when I discovered the signal. Tracking it revealed the location. Other instruments enabled me to discover this man and his detector. With respect, sir, haste is all-important. I found one man but there could be others and the signal could even be picked up far into space.'

'I think that this is a matter for Security. They had better be notified.'

'A moment, sir.' Kennedy spoke quickly as the colonel reached for his intercom. 'This is no ordinary matter. There are certain involvements. The marshal is concerned, as well as his aide, Ipoh Luang. I dare say no more at this time, but if I give you the map references of the location I am sure that you will understand.' As the officer frowned he added, 'There are things, sir, of which you may be unaware. Believe me when I tell you that discretion now could offer high reward in the future.'

He had gone as far as he dared, but it was enough. Colonel Kwei was no fool and was fully aware of the political situation. And there had been rumors. If a spy had somehow managed to infiltrate into the upper echelons, then the less who knew about it the better. And the one who exposed him would be certain of promotion.

'You have proof of what you say?'

'I can give you a demonstration, sir. If you will arrange for a flier we can circle the location in question.'

'Very well.' Kwei glanced at Saratov as he reached toward his communicator. 'This man had better be placed under close arrest.'

'No, sir.' Kennedy was emphatic. 'Had that been wise it would already have been done. We need him to unmask the agent. And it would not be politic to allow him to talk.'

In the flier Kennedy relaxed a little. So far so good, but the hardest part was to come. As they circled the secret laboratory he switched on the detector which Saratov had made. The series of blips, each of a different note, come loud and clear. It was impossible for Kwei to know they came from the tiny transmitters in the stomachs of the melots; to him they sounded like a coded message.

As he listened the communicator burst into life.

'Calling the flier above. Identify yourself immediately.'

'Colonel Kwei on special mission.'

'You are over restricted territory. Explain your mission.'

Kennedy said as the colonel hesitated, 'Ask to speak to the highest authority. The marshal himself if possible.'

Kwei nodded and obeyed. The face on the screen vanished to be replaced by another.

'I am Ipoh Luang, aide to the marshal. He is not available, but you may speak fully to me.' He frowned as he listened, then came to the predicted decision. 'Land at once to make a personal report.'

The beam of a searchlight illuminated the ground well away from the building. As Kennedy had guessed, those within were taking no chances on another surprise attack; however, for the flier to land the alarms would have to be disconnected – and then Chemile would have his chance. Kennedy took his time leaving the flier. Saratov grunting as he dropped to the ground beside the impatient colonel.

'I don't know what all this is about,' Saratov complained. 'I'm just a harmless electronics amateur. I just made that thing for fun and you treat me like a criminal.'

'Shut your mouth!' Kwei drew his pistol from its holster and gestured with it toward the door. 'Move straight ahead and remain silent. Disobey and I will shoot!'

The door was an ordinary portal, a part of the disguise of the building, a slab of wood drawn back to show a short passage leading to a vestibule. Kennedy tensed as he neared it. Chemile would be standing to one side, invisible against the wall, but the interior held guards and before he could slip inside their attention had to be distracted. As the colonel neared the step, Kennedy hooked his foot and sent him sprawling. Immediately

Saratov sprang to one side, hands lifted, mouth open as he yelled at the top of his voice.

'Don't shoot me! I didn't do it! I'm innocent! Don't shoot me!'

A guard lunged forward, stumbling as Kennedy tripped over the colonel and slammed into him. For a moment all was confusion and, when order was restored, Chemile was safely inside.

Ipoh Luang waited in an inner room. He listened to the noise from the detector, then gave rapid orders. Men moved around with electronic equipment to determine the source of the transmission. As they left the room, Luang faced Kwei.

'You have done well, Colonel, and it will not be forgotten. However, I am sure that you have duties which demand your presence. It will be best that you attend to them. Again, my thanks; your name will be remembered.'

Kwei beamed, then glanced at Kennedy.

'The major will remain together with his prisoner,' Luang said. 'Head directly back to the city, Colonel. And it would be wise for you to keep this incident to yourself.' As Kwei left, Luang said, casually, 'And now, Major, let us find out just who and what you are.'

'I don't understand.'

'No?' Luang leaned back in his chair, smiling. 'You do not strike me as an unintelligent man. Surely I made myself plain.'

Kennedy said, stiffly, 'I am Major Yeni of the communications corps.'

'Of course.' Luang was bland. 'But it seems a little odd to me that you should have come here at just this time. Looking for the marshal, perhaps? Well, never mind, all will be known in good time. Later I will question you. Until then you will remain here as my guest.' He touched a button on his desk and to the guards who answered the summons said, 'Take them below.'

The cells were small, iron bars reaching from floor to roof, each holding a narrow cot devoid of covers. Kell bulbs threw a blue radiance and the air smelled of damp and the acrid odor of animals. A single guard paced the corridor and from somewhere came the sound of a man in pain.

Saratov whispered, 'I could spring these bars, Cap. Shall I do it?'

'Later.' Action without a plan was useless. 'We're inside and so is Veem. We can afford to wait.'

Wait and watch as the guard paced by, timing his journeys,

noting little eccentricities. The way he drifted toward his left, how he held his club, his stolid indifference toward those he guarded. Information which could later be put to use.

Kennedy lay on the cot, head resting on his hands, eyes fixed on the ceiling. An hour passed, time enough for Chemile to have roamed the building, deciding on the weak spots and discovering the whereabouts of the laboratory.

Suddenly boots rasped on the concrete floor, bars clashed as doors were thrown open, and sharp voices snapped commands.

Ipoh Luang came down the corridor. Halting before Kennedy's cell, he waved away the guards and stood for a moment, eyes shadowed. Then he smiled.

'It would seem, my friend, that you are a liar.'

Kennedy rose from his cot but remainined silent, recognizing the smile for what it was. The grimace of a sadist anticipating pleasure.

'Major Yeni is on duty at his station. I have checked his identity and verified his movements over the past two days. I tell you this so that you will waste no more time in futile pretense. Also, I have discovered the source of those mysterious signals.'

He waited, expecting a response, and when none came he snapped, 'You will tell me how those transmitters were introduced into the stomachs of the melots. And you will tell me every detail of the plot which brought you here.'

Kennedy shrugged.

'You refuse to answer? That was anticipated, but let me warn you that we have means of making even the stones cry out. Cooperate and you will avoid a great deal of unpleasantness. In fact, you could gain a high reward.'

Saratov said loudly, 'Let me out, sir. I've nothing to do with all this. I was just given that detector and told to keep my mouth shut. On Merah we have to obey an officer.'

Without turning his head, Luang said, 'Guard!'

The man came forward, club lifted, savagely prodding. Saratov fell, whimpering, a grossly fat man incapable of harm.

'You remain silent,' said Luang to Kennedy. 'Perhaps you are hoping that you will be rescued. Or that another attack will be made and our positions reversed. That will not happen. The man you had standing by with a flier is now under arrest. An old man and one, I think, who will be more amenable to interrogation. We shall see. In the meantime I shall allow you to

98

hear his screams. Think of him when you do. It may help to loosen your tongue.'

Luang turned and strode away, the attendant guards following, except for the cell-guard. As he walked his beat to the end of the passage, Saratov whispered, 'Cap! They've got Jarl!'

Luden had flown Chemile to the area and had waited in what he thought was a safe place. His capture altered the situation. Now he could no longer create an external distraction by the use of catapulted explosives timed to detonate at irregular intervals. The distraction for which Kennedy had waited, intending to wreck the laboratory under cover of the confusion it would cause.

'Cap!' Saratov was anxious. 'We can't let them torture Jarl.'

'A moment, Penza.'

They still had time to spare, and to act precipitately would ruin their chance. Luang had said they would hear screams, which meant doors would be opened to allow the passage of sound. That very sound would guide them to where they had to go and it would drown out other noises which might arouse attention. Luden had a low pain tolerance and had no mistaken ideas as to the value of silence under torture. Those applying it wanted to hear screams and he would willingly oblige.

The first one came as the guard came level with Kennedy's cell. He paused, grinning, unmindful of his unconscious drift to the side which had brought him within arm's reach. He lost his grin as Kennedy's fingers closed on his wrist and jerked him hard against the bars. He slumped beneath the stabbing impact of stiffened fingers.

'Penza!'

Saratov was already at work. His great hands clamped around the bars of the door as his foot lifted to rest against the cage. Cloth ripped across his shoulders as he strained. The snap of the lock was drowned in another yell from beyond the corridor. Before it was repeated Kennedy was free and running down the corridor with the giant at his heels.

A guard stood at the far end. He opened his mouth to shout a warning, then doubled up, retching blood as Kennedy's hand slammed across his throat. Another died beneath the hammer-impact of Saratov's clenched fist. More yells guided them to a room with an open door through which they could see a figure strapped in a chair, instruments, two white-coated technicians,

99

and the gloating face of Ipoh Luang.

It changed as he saw Kennedy, becoming strained, frightened, the eyes wide as he clawed at his holstered pistol. But Kennedy was on Luang before he could draw the weapon, one hand reaching, catching the wrist, twisting with trained, instinctive skill. Bone snapped and Luang screamed as the jagged ends grated together. He screamed again as he saw the hand raised above his eyes, the edge smashing down at the bridge of his nose.

'Cap!' Saratov had taken care of the others, smashing them down with crushing blows, hurling them to slam against the walls. 'Cap!'

Kennedy looked at the frail shape in the chair, the pale face with blood on the mouth. Unconsciously his hand tightened on Luang's throat, murderous rage rising at the thought of what the creature had done and intended to do. A sadist with the power to release the beast in all of humanity. Once started, where would he stop?

'Cap!' said Saratov again. He pulled at Kennedy's arm. 'Your face, Cap! Let him go. He's dead.'

Kennedy rose. Thickly he said, 'How's Jarl?'

'Alive,' said Luden precisely as the giant released him from the straps. 'Though at times I had cause to wish I wasn't.' Carefully he touched his mouth. 'I had never realized that the dental nerves were so sensitive and capable of causing so much discomfort. When I think of what the early peoples had to suffer under primitive surgery I am filled with admiration at their fortitude.'

'Never mind that, Jarl. Can you walk?'

'Certainly I can walk. They worked on my mouth, not my feet.' Jarl rose and then said, quietly, 'But, Cap I don't think that we will walk very far.'

Guards were at the door, Diones leveled, behind them the tall figure of Ser Prome. He looked dispassionately at the carnage.

'A typical product of the emotional reaction of unthinking animals,' he said. 'I should not have to warn you to make no hostile moves. If one of you offers resistance all will be burned without hesitation. You!' He pointed to Saratov. 'Step forward and halt before me.'

The Chambodian held a hypogun in one clawlike hand. As the giant paused he lifted it and fired at Saratov's throat. The air-blast sounded like a muffled cough as it carried the dose through cloth and skin and fat into the bloodstream.

'Pass down the corridor and wait at the far end. If you resist or refuse to obey, your companions will die. And now you.' The Chambodian pointed at Luden.

Kennedy hesitated when his turn came, but there was nothing he could do. To resist was to die and take the others with him. He felt the blast of the drug and moved to join the others. At least Luang was dead and perhaps Chemile could finish the job.

'The marshal is a fool,' said Ser Prome. 'You will find him beyond the door you are facing and through which you will shortly pass. But his stupidity was minor compared to that of his aide. Luang deserved to die, but his passing is inconvenient to my plans. He should have known, as I know, that you are not the representatives of the local plot, but his desire for personal aggrandizement blinded him to the obvious. As soon as I learned that the drug had been used on Terra I foresaw what must inevitably happen. Steps could have been taken against it, but the cabal was torn by dissension. Well, no matter. I alone have the secret and it can be used again on some other world. I leave you with that thought. That you, the agents of Terra, have utterly failed in your mission.'

It was unlike Chambodians to boast, but his contempt of what he regarded as a lesser race had loosened Ser Prome's tongue. And it was gratifying to salvage something at least from the wreck of his plans.

'It would, of course, be possible to reestablish the operation, but with Luang dead it would take too long to reach a new equilibrium. And I am not so foolish as to suppose that there will be no other agents to replace you. Perhaps they will find you, but I think it most unlikely. Within a short while you will all be dead.'

'Murdered,' said Kennedy. 'What's the matter, Chambodian? Are you too squeamish to call things what they are?'

'Not murdered. I shall not touch you nor will the guards. You came to discover the secret of the drug; well, you have found it. It has been injected into your blood. Now pass through that door and wait for death to come to you, one against the other like the beasts you are!'

CHAPTER FOURTEEN

Bassein looked up as they entered. He sat at a small table, his elbows on the surface, his head in his hands. Dully he said, 'I heard. You came too late.'

'You?'

'I tried to warn Terra. It was the only way I could. Aihun Zemao had the drug with orders to make tests.' Bassein licked his dry lips. His face was haggard, creased with remembered pain. 'They tortured me,' he whispered. 'Then put me in here. The Chambodian injected me as he did you.'

It was impossible to feel pity for the man. Kennedy looked down at him, remembering Justine, his family, the dead girl, the riot, the others who had died for the sake of an insane dream. Killed by the mind-death this planet had produced, the death which even now was in his blood.

Luden said, sharply, 'Sit down, Cap. You too, Penza. On no account must any of us yield to the urgings of emotion. When the drug takes effect we shall be balanced on a razor's edge. It is imperative that we keep calm and detached.'

'That is easier said than done, Jarl.'

'We must do it. Emotions will become magnified and actions performed without conscious volition. For example, you have a habit of tweaking your ear, Penza. I find it a little irritating, but normally it does not worry me. Now that I have been injected with the drug that irritation could develop into a murderous rage. In that case I shall try to kill you.'

'You think you could do it, Jarl?'

'I couldn't, but I will still try. In return you will be unable to control your resistance to my attack. You will kill me, then Cap will try to kill you, and so on. We must remain calm at all times.'

Bassein raised his head again. 'I'm sorry,' he said. 'You must believe that. But I did try to warn you.'

102

'Why?' All information was of value and Kennedy was thinking of the future. 'You were Marshal of Merah. You could have stopped this had you tried. Why try to warn us of what you intended?'

'You don't understand. I was against strong opposition – Luang, others. They would have deposed me and nothing would have been gained. It was better that a few died than no warning should have been given. You see that, surely? There was nothing else I could have done.'

They didn't understand. Bassein read their faces, the cold hostility, the naked anger. *They will kill me*, he thought. *Very soon now they will forget they are civilized and vent their hatred on my body*. And there was no escape, the door had been locked behind them. Ser Prome's idea of humor, perhaps, letting the monkey-men he despised rip each other apart.

He felt tears run down his cheeks. He was old, too old. That girl had almost said it. What was her name? Gyma ... Glida ... he couldn't remember. Another failure to add to the rest. The obvious trap into which he had fallen, his choice of allies, even the Chambodian, all bad errors of judgement. Depression came over him in a crushing wave. He was a failure and never had been anything else. He had caused innocent people to die because he had been too great a coward to face the necessity of what had to be done, relying instead on others to negate his lack of firm decision. He felt shame at the way he had screamed during the interrogation. More cowardice; a soldier should be able to stand pain. And these men knew it. He felt their contempt, their scorn. He had to escape. He had to escape!

Rising, he went to the door, twisted the knob, turning as the panel held fast. Inside him self-hatred grew like a fungus. If he had carried a gun he would have shot himself, but he had no gun. No gun, no knife, nothing; but the wall was made of concrete, the room wide. He lunged at it, head lowered, running as he struck. He was a heavy man. The sound of his breaking skull was like the squash of a melon.

'Cap!' Luden's voice was low, evenly modulated. 'Sit down. You can do nothing for the man. He is dead.'

Saratov said, 'Why did he kill himself?'

'For escape, perhaps. When pressures become too great there is always suicide. Don't think of it, Penza. Look at the table, study the grain, concentrate on minute sections and forget that you aren't alone. There is beauty in the grain of wood. Follow the lines and note the complexities. From now on it would be best if we didn't speak to each other. Sometimes a word can arouse antagonism.'

Kennedy relaxed, breathing deeply, slowly. The hard-learned Clume Discipline would give him mastery of his body, but would it enable him to control the urgings of the subconscious? It was a risk he chose not to take, using instead the Ghergach System of Disorientation which expanded his mental parameters and gave a cool detachment. Luden himself with the trained emotional discipline of years was no problem even if he had been physically strong. Saratov was the real danger. If the giant machine of his body should run amok he could kill them both.

For a long time he stared at the table, twitching a little, small tremors running beneath his skin. He said, 'How long, Jarl?'

'Talking is not advisable, Penza.'

'Giving me orders, you skinny freak? I asked a question. Answer it!'

'We have already assimilated the drug,' said Luden patiently. His face suddenly contorted with anger, teeth bared between snarling lips. With an effort he controlled himself and Kennedy could see beads of sweat on the high forehead.

Quickly Kennedy said, 'The Hammarand Formula, Jarl. Have you extrapolated the final steps?'

Luden looked at his hands. They were curved, the fingers hooked like claws ready to rip and tear. Deliberately he straightened them, concentrating on the enigmatic mystery of an equation found on a barren world. In the dispassionate realm of mathematics he could find emotional safety.

Saratov had no such relief. The energy which powered his mighty frame demanded release; unless faced with a job of work he was restless, which was one of the reasons why he bickered with Chemile.

Rising, he began to pace the floor. Kennedy watched him, feeling a growing irritation. Saratov's feet were too heavy and he made too much noise. Incipient violence hung around him like a cloud disturbing his mental disorientation. As he passed his thigh hit the table and he demolished it with a smashing blow of his clenched fist. A fragment hit Luden on the cheek and he rose, hands lifted, eyes blazing.

'You big, stupid fool! Sit down!'

Penza roared and lunged forward.

Kennedy rose, kicking back his chair, thrusting himself between the two. Luden staggered to one side from the impact of his body as Saratov clamped his giant hands around Kennedy's throat. The fingers were like steel.

'You!' he snarled. 'You!'

Kennedy felt a rising tide of anger, a primitive rage which tore at the careful mental discipline he had so painstakingly achieved. He wanted to fight, to kill, to tear at the hands and beat at the giant body without thought of injury or possible death. To do what Ser Prome had confidently anticipated. Instead he relaxed.

Only the Ghergach System of Disorientation enabled him to do it: to keep his hands hanging loose at his sides, his muscles limp. To resist would be to add fuel to Saratov's rage, to fight would be to trigger an overwhelming, unthinking reaction.

He felt the hands tighten, then saw the giant's eyes, the struggle they held, the mute appeal.

'Penza,' he said. 'The door.'

His rage could not be contained, but it could be directed, and Kennedy knew that his own restraint was weakening. No discipline, no matter how applied, could be stronger than the primeval heritage carried in the subconscious mind.

The hands eased a little. 'Cap?'

'The door,' said Kennedy again. 'Our enemies are out there.'

The hands fell away as Saratov thrust the weight of his body like a battering ram against the panel. Lock and hinges burst, slamming the door back into the passage, crushing those who had stood outside eager to hear the sounds of murder. Kennedy sprang forward, snatched up a Dione, triggered it as he spun, snarling. A man shrieked as the incandescent beam charred a hole through his intestines. Another turned to run and fell, smoke rising from his skull. Luden joined in together with Saratov. Within seconds the corridor was clear.

Like three demons they raced through the lower part of the building. They were more than demons. They were the most terrible life-form the galaxy had ever known . . . members of a race which had fought from mud to the stars, whose every page of history was stained with blood . . . creatures determined to survive and now utterly without restraint.

Guards tried to stop them and were burned down. Others ran. A man could hope to avoid a bullet and live if struck, but the searing flame of a Dione was not easy to face. Especially when it came from guns held before snarling faces more vicious than the flame itself.

Kennedy saw a shape lean over the parapet of an upper stair. He fired with instinctive aim, heard the scream and the thud of a falling body. Roaring, Saratov smashed through a locked door, threw himself at the men beyond, forgetting his gun in the frenzy which gripped him. Bones snapped, skulls spouted blood and brain, like limp dolls the guards were flung aside.

Kennedy fired at others beyond, heard the thunder of Luden's weapon as he took care of those edging behind. The air stank of blood and charred flesh.

'Up!' Kennedy threw aside his empty gun and reached for another lying beside a crumpled figure. For a moment he had yielded to the savage joy of uncontrolled violence, but there was work to be done. 'The laboratory. The Chambodian.'

He led the way up the stairs. A handful of guards had clustered at the head, determined to make a stand. They were nervous and fired too soon and too carelessly. Shafts of ravening energy lanced over Kennedy's head as he ducked, firing in return. A man spun, gaping at the blood spouting from a severed arm. Another fell with a hole charred over the region of his heart. Two more toppled beneath the concentrated fire of the others. The fire continued as they mounted the stairs, a bath of flame in which nothing living could survive.

'We could get them all,' boomed Saratov. 'Clean out the entire building of these scum!'

The giant was a mess of blood, blisters on the side of his shaven head, more marring the smooth line of his shoulders. Luden was little better. His gray hair was crisped and ash mottled his cheek.

'Cap!' Luden reached out and caught Kennedy by the arm. 'Don't forget that Veem's in here somewhere.'

Kennedy shook his head and took a deep breath. Some of the madness had left him, the insane fury of rage which had carried them so far. The effect of the drug, he guessed, must be wearing off, but his determination remained to destroy the threat to civilized man.

He looked around. A short passage led from the head of the stair to a closed door. No guards were in sight, but he guessed that some must remain and one alone, using gas or firing from

106

concealment, could cut them down. Before that happened their mission had to be accomplished.

'That door,' he said. 'Penza!'

It flew open beneath the slam of the giant's boot. Beyond lay a long, wide room filled with chemical apparatus, metal and crystal bright beneath rows of lights. Cages stood empty to one side of an operating table and shelves were lined with containers of chemicals. Sealed vials stood on a bench, each marked with the Meraninian death-symbol. The drug, perhaps? There was no way of telling and no one to ask. The laboratory appeared deserted.

Then a portion of the wall seemed to shift, to step forward in the shape of a man.

'Veem!' Saratov's voice boomed from the walls. 'You're safe! I was worried about you!'

'I heard the shooting,' said Chemile. 'You make a large target, Penza. I'm glad to see they missed.' He leaned against a bench, looking tired, his skin a mass of drifting color as he relaxed conscious control. 'I've had a hard time. Guards seemed to be everywhere and I had to be careful, but I found out a few things. This is where they make the drug. The Chambodian cleared everyone out when you were arrested.'

Kennedy said, 'Do you know where he is?'

'He's got a small apartment under the roof. I didn't have much time to inspect it. The big Dione is on a pneumatic platform, but they won't be able to use it now. I jammed the controls. I fixed the other guns too.'

Chemile had been busy. Kennedy looked around and saw a compact incinerator, probably used for the disposal of dead melots.

'Guard the door, Penza. Jarl, help me throw those containers into the incinerator.'

As they worked Chemile said, 'There's no need for that, Cap. There's enough chemicals here to stock a factory. I used some to make a couple of bombs. They're powerful enough to turn this whole building into dust.'

'Timed?'

'Ten minutes from when we throw the trigger.'

Too long to take a chance. Kennedy threw the last of the vials into the incinerator, slammed the lid, and waited until they had been reduced to harmless vapors. From the door Penza said,

'Trouble, Cap. They're bringing up a shielded projector.'

It stood at the head of the stairs, the tough shield proof against the impact of missiles and the flame of hand-Diones. Men crouched behind it, nervous under the snap of an officer sheltering on the stairs. Fired, it would blast the laboratory with a hail of exploding destruction.

'The muzzle,' snapped Kennedy. 'Concentrated fire.'

The one weak point of the weapon, a small target but vulnerable. Lifting his Dione, Kennedy sent a shaft of raw energy blasting against the orifice. Metal glowed red beneath the impact. He fired again, the others joining in. The air in the passage grew hot, scorching to the lungs, the men behind the shield wincing to the glow of heated metal. White-hot, the muzzle began to drip a molten rain, blocking the aperture through which the missiles had to pass. Their nerve broken, the guards ran down the stairs.

'Done it.' Saratov lowered his weapon. 'But why didn't they fire?'

'Because it was quite unnecessary,' said a cold voice behind them. 'I have no wish to see my laboratory destroyed. No! Do not turn! Drop your guns and stand immobile.' Ser Prome drew in his breath as they obeyed. 'That is better. Now you may face me.'

He stood very tall, the gun in his hand unwavering as it pointed at the three men.

'Animals,' he sneered. 'Unthinking beasts. You should have been destroyed at once.'

'A mistake,' said Kennedy. 'You underestimated us. That fault, Chambodian, is often fatal.'

'You threaten me?' The tall figure shrugged. 'I find that incredible. You are trapped in this laboratory, and even if you broke free you have still to escape from the building. Even now guards are on their way to take you and, let me assure you, you will not escape again.'

'This room was empty,' said Luden. 'How did you get here? A secret panel leading from your apartment?'

'For an animal you are shrewd.'

Kennedy ignored the insult, his eyes searching the walls. Chemile was nowhere to be seen, yet he had to be close. Unarmed, he could not have helped with the destruction of the gun and so had managed to render himself invisible as the Chambodian had come through his panel. Now Chemile appeared beside a bench, stooped beneath it, rose, and crept up behind Ser Prome. Slipping his hand beneath the other arm, he knocked up the gun.

'I've triggered the bombs,' he said as Kennedy grabbed the tall figure. 'We'll have to get out of here, Cap.'

'How?' roared Saratov. 'Veem, you fool, you'll blow us all to dust!'

'The panel.' Chemile crossed to where a chart hung against the wall. 'It's behind this. I saw him come through it.'

It led to a stair, to a small apartment from which another stair led below. Guards stood at the bottom, to die in the blast of roaring guns. But their reputation had preceded them and as Kennedy led the way to the door other guards scattered, throwing aside their weapons, running to escape the killing fury which had taken so many of their number.

Firmly held in Saratov's big arms, Ser Prome writhed in impotent anger. 'Animals! How dare you lay hands on one of my race! Beasts in the shape of men, let me go!'

'Shut up!' growled the giant. 'Cap!'

An officer, more courageous or more stupid than his men, barred their way. He held a rapid-fire projector, lifting it as they appeared, finger tightening to send a stream of missiles lancing toward them. Kennedy hit the floor, felt the thuds as the others followed suit, then fired as explosions blasted the walls and floor behind. The single shot was enough. The officer fell, his face a charred ruin, blood seeping from the hole between his eyes.

'Out!' Kennedy led the way to the door, tore it open, then turned to cover the others as they ran outside. Night closed around them, grass soft beneath their feet as they headed toward the river. As they reached it a glare of light rose from the building.

'The bombs!' Luden shook his head. 'You miss-timed, Veem.' He ducked as more explosions followed the first.

'The guns,' said Chemile. 'The arsenal.' He looked at the devastation, light painting streamers of shifting color on his face. 'Well, Cap, that's taken care of the problem.'

Not quite. Kennedy looked at the Chambodian. In his mind still rested the secret of the mind-death, the hatred of mankind which would make him use it. Slowly he lifted his hand, the gun it contained.

'Let him go, Penza.'

As he obeyed the giant said, 'Let me do it, Cap.'

'Do what?' The Chambodian stood against the burning build-ing, his hawk-face wreathed in a nimbus of light. 'Do you intend to take me prisoner? You have no jurisdiction here. Or is it your intention to let this animal serve as your assassin?'

'No.' Kennedy would never delegate unwelcome responsi-bility. He said, formally, 'Ser Prome, as a Free Acting Terran Envoy endowed with full authority to maintain the *Pax Terra* I find you guilty of the crime of murder against various mem-bers of my race. From your own words and actions stated and performed before witnesses it is clear that you will continue to use your discovery to compound those murders. In view of the circumstances I have no choice but – '

'Is this farce a trial?'

'No,' said Kennedy flatly. 'Not a trial.'

Ser Prome read his death in Kennedy's eyes. He stood for a moment as if thinking and then, abruptly, turned and ran toward the burning building, his hand thrust into his robe. He spun, lift-ing his hand and hurling something which shot a humming sparkle toward the little group. Kennedy fired, hitting it, releas-ing a flood of destructive energy which would have destroyed them all. He fired again, a third time, closing his finger as the accredited executioner of Terran Control.

Like a candle the Chambodian, already dead, stood in a mantle of flame.

Another title in the **MEWS** series

F.A.T.E. 1:
Galaxy of the Lost

by Gregory Kern

Captain Kennedy, Earth's trouble shooter, carries
the Banner of Terran against the unknown sciences
and alien psychologies of a thousand worlds.

The crack in the cosmos that has to be sealed!

F.A.T.E. is the space hero series that has become a
must wherever Science Fiction is read. A solid space
adventure more exciting than 'Startrek' and far more
real than 'Perry Rhodan'.

On sale at newsagents and booksellers everywhere.

MEWS BESTSELLERS

R 9   JOHN EAGLE 1: NEEDLES OF DEATH   *Paul Edwards* 40p

R 17   SATAN SLEUTH 1: FALLEN ANGEL   *Michael Avallone* 40p

R 25   SPIDER 1: DEATH REIGN OF THE VAMPIRE KING
                                          Grant Stockbridge 40p

R 92   SPIDER 2: HORDES OF THE RED BUTCHER
                                          Grant Stockbridge 40p

R 33   FATE 1: GALAXY OF THE LOST   *Gregory Kern* 40p

R106   FATE 2: SLAVESHIP FROM SERGAN   *Gregory Kern* 40p

R 41   JAMES GUNN 1: THE DEADLY STRANGER
                                          John Delaney 40p

R 68   CHURCHILL'S VIXENS 1: THE BRETON BUTCHER
                                          Leslie McManus 40p

R114   CHURCHILL'S VIXENS 2: THE BELGIAN FOX
                                          Leslie McManus 40p

R 76   THE BIG BRAIN 1: THE AARDVARK AFFAIR
                                          Gary Brandner 40p

R 84   THE CRAFT OF TERROR   *Ed. Peter Haining* 40p

R122   BLACK SCARAB   *Norman Gant* 40p

NEL P.O. BOX 11, FALMOUTH, TR10 9EN, CORNWALL.

For U.K.: Customers should include to cover postage, 18p for the first book plus 8p per copy for each additional book ordered up to a maximum charge of 66p.

For B.F.P.O. and Eire: Customers should include to cover postage, 18p for the first book plus 8p per copy for the next 6 and thereafter 3p per book.

For Overseas: Customers should include to cover postage, 20p for the first book plus 10p per copy for each additional book.

Name ....

Address ....

....

....

Title ....

Whilst every effort is made to maintain prices, new editions or printings may carry an increased price and the actual price of the edition supplied will apply.